# Down Pans Lane

The history of
Roundway Hospital, Devizes
1851 - 1995

*Philip Steele*

with Appendix by
Geoff Mascall

Published in 2000 by

Philip Steele
19B Frome Road
Bradford on Avon
Wilts  BA15 2EA


Cover Illustrations by Valerie Bowyer


Appendix by Geoff Mascall


Typeset in 10/12 Book Antiqua


Design and typesetting by
Dave Steele Mac Services
PO Box 1686
CV31 1WS


Printed by Redwood Books
Trowbridge

# Philip Steele

It was only in his retirement after thirty years as a Royal Air Force navigator and twelve as a local government officer that Philip Steele turned to researching and writing history. He took a BA honours degree in History with English, and then an MA in Local and Regional History, both at the Bath Spa University College, a convenient distance from his home in Bradford on Avon. His first topics as a budding historian were in the field of air navigation history, in association with the Royal Institute of Navigation. He was elected a Fellow of that Institute in 1997, and was awarded its 1998 Bronze Medal for the best article in *The Journal of Navigation*. Seeking a local subject for his MA dissertation, he was introduced by the staff of the Wiltshire and Swindon Record Office to its comprehensive set of records of the recently-closed Roundway Hospital, going back to its opening as the Wiltshire County Asylum in 1851, and earlier. A complementary nugget of source material soon came to his attention at the Wiltshire Archaeological and Natural History Society's library in Devizes, where it became clear that there was a real need for someone to write the Hospital's full story. The rest, as they say, is history.

# Contents

*View of Roundway Hospital used in **Roundway Review**, 1950s.*

# Preface

A book which recounts a piece of local history for local consumption needs to be very different from an academic dissertation. Yet it was as a dissertation that this book started its life. The need to make a dissertation authentic, interesting and informative can get in the way of another important aim, making it 'a good read'. I have tried to promote this quality firstly by stripping out the daunting 'academic apparatus' of indexing and referencing, while retaining the material's authority and the due credit given to my sources. Secondly, I have tried, and have very much enjoyed the process, to give freer rein to the mass of material which had to be left out of the dissertation, because it would have made it too anecdotal or too long.

Rather than use footnotes or end notes, as far as is practical I have indicated sources in the text. Where there are direct quotations, I have named the author and the title of the book or article. It can be assumed that any quotations for which I have not given the source in this way are from the sequence of official records - annual reports, committee minutes, case books and associated documents - held by the Wiltshire and Swindon Record Office (WRO) in Trowbridge and by the Wiltshire Archaeological and Natural History Society (WANHS) in Devizes. For any reader who would like to narrow the sources down to precise documents and page numbers, copies of my original dissertation, fully referenced and entitled *Life-Cycle of a County Mental Hospital*, are available for consultation at WANHS, at the Wiltshire County Local Studies Library in Trowbridge, and at Bath Spa University College.

A word about the pictures on the cover and between chapters. They are reproduced, with her permission and valued assistance, from paintings by Valerie Bowyer, who lives in Bradford on Avon and has frequently exhibited locally. They are from a set which she felt moved to paint when, in November 1995 she passed the deserted Roundway Hospital buildings, once the source of great civic pride, and was struck by their desolation, and by the emptiness and distress, built up over the years. She felt a personal challenge to capture the atmosphere, the delapidations, and at the same time the care that thousands of confused souls had received during the lifetime of the Hospital.

As regards the other illustrations, I am grateful to a range of sources. I acknowledge with thanks the permission given by Pamela Colman, John Leech, David Buxton and John Girvan, to reproduce photographs from their published books, and to the WRO for allowing me to use photographs and copies of archive material. My thanks to Dr Don Early, for permission to photograph exhibits at the Glenside Hospital Museum, Bristol. Thanks also to Chris Nicholson of Pinecraven Homes, and also to Joan Bradley and Peggy Hancock, for permission to reproduce pictures, and to Gweneth Helliar and to Bill and Bridget Styche for the use of their newspaper cuttings. In the latter case I am most grateful also to the Editors of the *Wiltshire Gazette and Herald* and the *Wiltshire Times* for waiving any relevant copyright formalities.

I am grateful to a large number of people for their assistance in many different ways. Prominent among these are the staff at the WRO under their Principal Archivist, John d'Arcy, the WANHS librarians Pamela Colman (now retired) and Lorna Haycock, and those who shared their own recollections of Roundway Hospital; Rev Geoffrey Barton, Angela Bassett, Reginald Buttery, Ann Chapman, Rosemary Colyer (with particular thanks for safeguarding the post-1974 National Health Service records), Chris Cox, BC, Ann Eccles, Bill Greenaway, James Harrison, Gweneth Helliar, Douglas Hodder, John Leech, Catherine Leigh, Dr George Lodge, Geoff Mascall, Peter Nolan, Bill Styche, Bridget (Melody) Styche, Ann Thompson and DW. Thanks are due also to Roy Luck of Consilium Construction for allowing access to the former Roundway site, and to David Steele for computer advice and services. The help and support is gratefully acknowledged of the tutorial staff in the History Department of Bath Spa University College, notably those most directly concerned with my MA studies in Local and Regional History, Dr Graham Davis and Dr Penny Bonsall.

Finally, my thanks go to the League of Friends of Green Lane Hospital for their offer of help in publicising this book. I have undertaken with great pleasure to donate to them any profits which might accrue from the project.

# 1 - Kindliness and Vigilance

Late in 1853, Dr John Thurnam wrote his third Annual Report as Medical Superintendent of the Wiltshire County Asylum. His first two reports had necessarily dealt mainly with the mundane processes of getting the Asylum established and running. But he was able now to broaden the scope, by including a summary of historical attitudes to lunacy, and an outline of the modern methods of treatment, in the development of which he himself had played a significant part.

Thurnam quoted Shakespeare's reference to 'the madhouse and the whip', and Swift's to 'phlebotomy, and whips, and dark chambers, and straw. He cited London's Bethlem Hospital ('Bedlam') in the eighteenth century, where 'the poor patient, maltreated, neglected, and abandoned to the indulgence of every wayward impulse, was presented as a common show to the gaze of the ignorant and the unfeeling'. These were practices which 'in the present day we

*By permission of John Leech*
**Dr John Thurnam**

1

should incline to suppose could exist only in a barbarous age'. He noted the introduction of more humane methods by both Philippe Pinel at the Bicêtre in Paris and also, 'in entire ignorance of Pinel's work', by William Tuke at the Quaker Retreat in York, late in the eighteenth century. Pinel had released 'from chains and darkness' more than fifty 'dangerous' lunatics, and his *Treatise on Insanity* breathed 'an admirable spirit of genuine good sense and philanthropy'. Nearly as important, Thurnam felt, was the *Description of the Retreat* written by Samuel Tuke, grandson of the York institution's founder.

A Quaker himself and born near York, Thurnam had first-hand experience of the York Retreat. After four years at Westminster Hospital he had returned to York and spent the eleven years before his Wiltshire appointment as the first medically-qualified Superintendent of the Retreat, and while there had published some well-respected observations and statistics on lunacy. 'From the first', he now wrote:

> all harsh and violent methods were there discarded, and it was soon found, by kindliness and vigilance, by ingenious arts of diversion and occupation, to how great an extent order might be maintained, confidence secured, and recovery promoted.

The 'Quaker system of management' had been studied widely in England and in Europe, and:

> by the light thus obtained, abuses were reformed in old asylums, legislative enactments were pressed forward, and the committees and officers of County Asylums, about this time first established, sought instruction within the walls of the Retreat at York.

It had been thought, even at York, that mechanical restraint might always be needed in some cases, but Thurnam credits Dr Charlesworth, at Lincoln Asylum during the 1820s, with the bold step of abandoning such restraint completely, despite opposition from 'older practitioners' and 'much public discussion and clamour'. Other institutions, notably the Middlesex Asylum under Dr Conolly, followed Lincoln's example, until by the 1850s there was 'scarcely a public asylum in the kingdom ... in which such restraint is resorted to, unless in very rare instances'. Thurnam pledged that in the Wiltshire County Asylum 'personal restraint is never resorted to, and there is literally no strait waistcoat or any similar instrument of coercion in the institution'.

The policy in the Wiltshire Asylum was to provide 'a right moral treatment', consisting of 'constant surveillance of active and good-tempered attendants, who do all in their power to check the first appearance of excitement or impropriety', and direction to 'some useful occupation'. In cases of 'great violence' which could not be checked, 'temporary seclusion in a sleeping room is prescribed; or, for those requiring it, in a room, the walls and floor of which are padded, in order to prevent bodily injury. In some cases, exercise, in a quiet airing court, is sufficient to cut short the paroxysm.' If the patient were to undress persistently, or stay out of bed at night, 'his garments are secured on his person, by an ingeniously contrived button-lock. If he destroy his clothes or bedding, these are provided of strong materials - canvas, bed tick, or sail cloth - which may baffle the violence of the most destructive'. What Thurnam termed 'medical treatment' was required 'in every class of case ... to soothe an excited brain'. He had written while at York of the parallel value of 'pharmaceutical treament', but it must have played a minor role in the new Asylum, since the drugs bill in the early years (for 1853, £27 in a total budget of around £7000) was quite small. 'It is from a judicious combination of moral and therapeutic measures', he concludes, 'that the most satisfactory results are obtained'.

The treatment regime which Thurnam describes was part of a national trend, whose origins were perhaps rather broader than he indicates. Though the York Retreat is still acknowledged to have been the foremost of the institutions pioneering the new moral and kindly treatment, a few other voluntary asylums did exist in the late eighteenth century which had been set up by reformers and philanthropists with similar ideas. Roy Porter argues in *Mind-Forg'd Manacles* that 'much of what the nineteenth century claimed for its own had been established in the previous era', and that it is 'historically misleading' to claim a radical and sudden change of attitude and treatment around 1800 'from physical therapy to moral therapy, or from scandal to reform'.

Even in the notorious Bethlem Hospital, where the first record of insane patients dates from 1403, governors were by the mid-seventeenth century attending to the welfare of their patients, making frequent visits of inspection, and ordering in 1655 'that no officer or servant shall give any blows or ill language to any of the mad folks on pain of losing his place'. But visitors were admitted for a penny, right up to 1770, and under strict control even later; this was thought beneficial to the patients, but one writer stated, 'I saw a hundred spectators making sport of the miserable inhabitants, provoking them into furies of rage'. Porter argues that Bethlem's notoriety derived mainly from the fact that for several centuries it was unique; such scandals and abuses as it did have served as the 'bogey image of the bad old days and ways', becoming 'gold-dust to reformers'. As late as 1814, a House of Commons Select Committee reported that some patients there were chained by one arm to the wall, and naked except for a blanket. Padded cells, a humanitarian innovation first used thirty years before in Germany, were installed at Bethlem in 1844, just before they were incorporated into the design of the new Wiltshire Asylum.

The change in attitudes to the insane, and in their treatment, came by evolution rather than revolution. It represents not a change from brutality and neglect to benevolence and care, but a shift in the view of how insanity might best be dealt with. The old idea, Andrew Scull argues in *Social Order/Mental*

*Disorder*, was that the insane had lost the intellectual faculty that distinguishes man from beast, and therefore would respond only to crude coercion. Thus, in the view of a prominent seventeenth century physician, quoted by Courtney Dainton in *The Story of England's Hospitals*:

> Nothing is more necessary and more effective for the recovery of these people than forcing them to respect and fear intimidation. By this method the mind, held back by restraint, is induced to give up its arrogance and wild ideas and soon becomes meek and orderly. This is why maniacs often recover much sooner if they are treated with torture and treatment in hovels instead of with medicaments.

Scull describes in detail, as an example of the methods used at that time, the treatment used on George III:

> His body was immediately encased in a machine which left no liberty for motion. He was sometimes chained to a stake. He was frequently beaten and starved, and at best he was kept in subjection by menacing and violent language.

Francis Willis, for whom 'a great deal was at stake with this patient', dared to employ these methods because he considered they were the most likely to result in the King's recovery. Institutions practising many advanced ideas at the time were concurrently using cold plunge baths, handcuffs, blood-letting, induced vomiting, purgatives, and the draining of 'bad humours' through open sores.

The first Act for regulating madhouses was passed in 1774, and in 1808 came the Lunatics (Paupers or Criminals) Act, the first which gave poor-law authorities permissive powers to collect rates to fund public asylums. In 1828 there were two further Acts concerning lunatics; the County Lunatic Asylums Act empowered justices to erect county asylums for pauper and criminal lunatics, while the Madhouse Act repealed all earlier legislation and introduced licensing and strict conditions for houses where insane persons were looked after. Wiltshire was served at this time by asylums at Laverstock House, Salisbury; Fiddington House, Market Lavington; Fisherton House, Fisherton Anger; Kingsdown House, Box; Belle Vue House, Devizes; plus houses at Fonthill Gifford, and from 1833, Calne.

The Lunatics Act of 1845 had far-reaching effects. It set up a national Board of Commissioners in Lunacy, under the chairmanship of Lord Ashley, later to become the 7th Earl of Shaftesbury and the foremost social reformer of his day, who was to exercise great influence in this post until his death some forty years later. Existing licensed asylums were subjected to regular inspection by the Commissioners; an additional, sterner sanction to that provided by a local Committee of Visitors appointed by the Court of Quarter Sessions. Moreover, it directed Counties to provide an asylum for pauper lunatics, the spur which led to the building of the Wiltshire County Asylum.

# 2 - A Cheerful and Appropriate Appearance

At Wiltshire's 1846 Easter Sessions a Committee of Justices was formed, chaired by Sir John Wither Awdrey, 'either to superintend the erecting or providing an Asylum for the pauper Lunatics of the County of Wilts alone' or to join with others (county or borough) to provide a joint institution to meet the need. Its first inclinations were to respond at a leisurely pace and on a small scale. They asked the proprietors of the largest two licensed asylums in the County, Belle Vue House in Devizes and Fiddington House in Market Lavington, whether they would consider selling their houses and land to the County. At the time Belle Vue housed 182 paying and pauper patients, and Fiddington, with some overcrowding, 200. The total number of pauper lunatics in such facilities in the County was 220. But there were also some seventy housed in the Union workhouses and nearly 200 with families or friends; some of these would seek County Asylum places once they were available. Provision was needed, it was decided, for 250 places initially with the capability for later extension, and this demanded a site of at least forty acres. So though Mr Phillips of Belle Vue was willing to sell for £8500, and Mr Willett of Fiddington House for £14,000, neither place could provide an acceptable solution.

Some urgency was injected by the realisation that most neighbouring counties were already operating their own asylums, and by a clause in the Act empowering the Secretary of State, if a start was not made by August 1848, to cause an asylum to be built to his specification. The recommendation to erect an asylum was made in October 1847 and approved at the Hilary Quarter Session at Devizes on 4 January 1848. A Mr T H S Sotheron, who happened to be a member of the Committee of Justices, owned and was willing to sell a suitable site of 41 acres about a mile from the Devizes town centre, at the end of Pans Lane. The Committee bought this site for £6000, and by May 1848 had selected an architect's plan, drawn up by Messrs Wyatt & Brandon, which estimated a building cost of £25,476. The Secretary of State's approval of the project on 26 July just beat the deadline. The costs of land purchase, building and equipment were to be met by raising loans from a range of sources, including central government, to be defrayed over twenty-one years by a rate of three-farthings.

The Committee recommended Murhill stone for the external walls, 'having a more cheerful and appropriate Appearance than the heavy redbrick of the

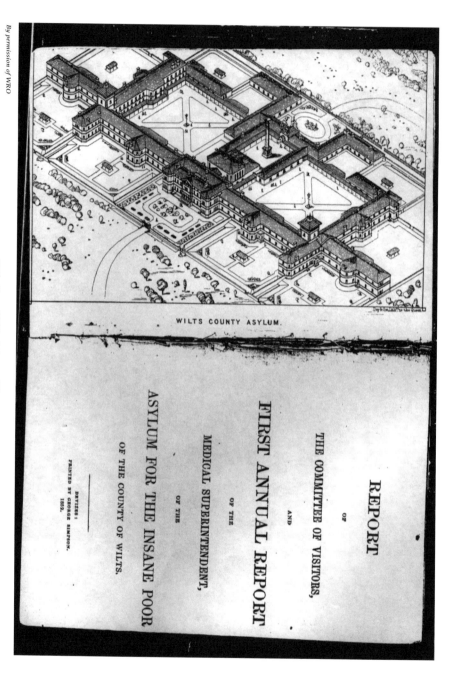

WILTS COUNTY ASYLUM.

REPORT

OF

THE COMMITTEE OF VISITORS,

AND

FIRST ANNUAL REPORT

OF THE

MEDICAL SUPERINTENDENT,

OF THE

ASYLUM FOR THE INSANE POOR

OF THE COUNTY OF WILTS.

DEVIZES:
PRINTED BY GEORGE SIMPSON,
1852.

*Title Page Of First Annual Report*

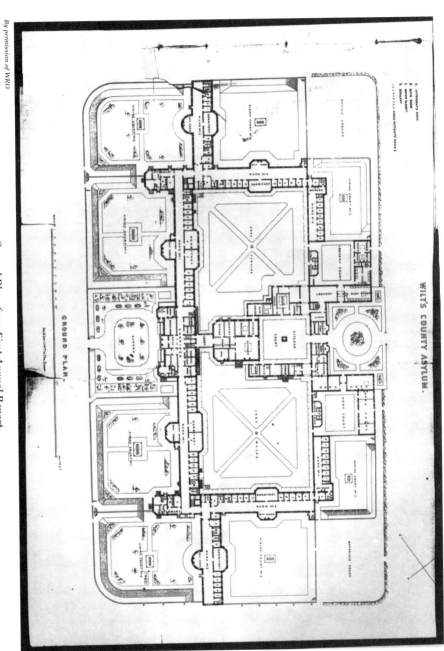

Ground Plan, from First Annual Report.

district'. It would be transported from the quarry, near Winsley, by way of the Kennet and Avon Canal. Though there was not yet a railway (the line near the Asylum was eventually opened in 1862), some members saw its likely proximity as a problem, though the majority thought it 'of no practical disadvantage, but rather an Object of Interest & Amusement to the patients'. They were pleased also to note that since many of the patients would be agricultural labourers, the need to find them practical occupation sat very well with the need to landscape the grounds and to create a farm, thus offering financial savings.

Further good financial news came with the acceptance of the tender from the builders Messrs T & W Piper at £19,594, plus ironwork at £1069 by Knight & Co, thus saving some £4000 on expected building costs. The construction process, started in summer 1849, seems to have gone smoothly, except for hold-ups arising from a labour dispute among those supplying the ironwork and from 'a vessel having been delayed in its voyage from Wales with the [roofing] slate, upwards of six weeks'. Ratepayers were less happy about the project; nearly 400 landowners, who 'contribute in a much larger degree to the County Rates than any other description of persons' unsuccessfully raised a petition against it. Though they felt 'the most anxious desire satisfactorily to provide for the Poor afflicted with insanity', they wanted it to remain 'the interest of individuals to treat them well' in private asylums, rather than the responsibility of public employees and ratepayers.

That the private asylums serving the County were far from adequate, however, is clear from the early national inspection reports of the Commissioners in Lunacy after 1845. At Fisherton House they found 'dirt and overcrowding', and at Kingsdown House, Box, 'mechanical restraint, including strait waistcoats, iron frames, hand locks, leg locks, and chains, used to an excessive degree, an inadequate staff, and the utmost uproar and excitement among the patients'. Belle Vue House in Devizes was singled out for particular castigation in the Commissioners' report for 1850. Its 'reprehensible' defects had 'repeatedly given great cause for dissatisfaction'; they included inadequate drainage, offensive privies, damp dormitories, refractory patients in dirty and ragged dresses, and inadequate washing facilities; these were due mainly to the failure of the proprietor, Mr Phillips, 'to expend a fair and sufficient sum for the care, clothing and maintenance of the paupers, in return for the payments made to him by the parishes'. There was a manifest need for a more efficient and sympathetic regime, as might be provided in a new Asylum.

The Wiltshire justices were fortunate in procuring the services as its Medical Superintendent of one as prominent in the development of the new approach as Dr Thurnam. He was appointed in March 1849, before construction was begun, and was thus able to advise throughout the process of building and equipping the institution. His advice on padded cells, furniture and kitchen equipment was accepted but his choice of flooring was considered too expensive. The Committee agreed with Thurnam that the number of inmates would increase; accordingly, an extension was incorporated in the building plan. This was to set a pattern of repeated extension which was to become a constant feature of the Asylum's history.

In May 1851 the building was far enough advanced for the Committee of Justices to hold its meeting there for the first time. In the same month, Thurnam was paid the first quarterly instalment of his £400-a-year salary, having previously been paid only expenses. The first patients were admitted on 19 September 1851.

The Wiltshire Justices' Committee of Visitors must have considered themselves fortunate to have secured the services of such an eminent figure in the treatment of lunacy as Dr John Thurnam. Why would he have chosen to come to Wiltshire, when such a wide choice of asylum posts was becoming available all around the country?

The answer may lie in his interest in the study of skulls, both ancient and modern, a science known as craniology or craniometry. As Colin Briden puts it in *Archaeological Papers from York*, 'Thurnam's everyday work led him to take a deep interest in what was passing inside his patients' heads: from this it was a small step to the study of the skull'. Thurnam, described in *The Dictionary of National Biography* as 'indefatigable in exploring ancient British barrows', had carried out several digs in Yorkshire, and the prospect of excavating some of Wiltshire's prehistoric sites must have been attractive to him. He would have foreseen the added benefit for this purpose of a potential workforce under his control - his patients, for whom he would need to find outdoor occupation as an essential part of the treatment regime in which he was such an ardent believer. Furthermore, he may have relished the prospect of collaborating with Dr Joseph Barnard Davis, who (as Peter Nolan has noted in a *Bulletin on the History of Nursing*) was living in Devizes at the time and who had amassed a vast collection of skulls - greater, in fact, than the sum of all the collections in British public museums.

Another possible clue to John Thurnam's attraction to Devizes is his marriage in June 1851, just before the Asylum opened, to Frances Elizabeth Wyatt, of a family characterised in the *Dictionary of National Biography* as 'prolific in artists and architects'. Her mother had been Anne Hillier of Devizes, and her brother Matthew (who became the Sir Matthew Digby Wyatt, architect of, among many notable buildings, Paddington Station) was born at Rowde, Devizes in 1820. Her eldest brother was Thomas Wyatt, the architect of Wiltshire's Asylum, and no doubt of other such institutions, since he was 'a consulting architect to the Lunacy Commissioners' and an 'acknowledged authority on hospital construction'. Thurnam could well have met Thomas Wyatt professionally in the course of his work while at the York Retreat, and through him, his sister Frances. On the other hand, since he was appointed to the Wiltshire post two years before his marriage, there would have been plenty of time for him to have met and courted Frances once he was in Wiltshire, even if he had not known her before.

Whatever the real reasons for Thurnam's choosing to come to Wiltshire, his appointment put the County in the forefront of developments in the treatment of insanity. Thurnam continued his craniological studies while at the Asylum, largely in partnership with Dr Davis, and published several works on the subject. His research, though in a field now largely discredited, has been acknowledged as 'a sure foundation for subsequent studies of insanity'. Making his mark at the national level, he became president of the Medico-Psychological Institution, but his contemporaries appear to have had mixed feelings about him, some showing particular scorn for his hasty and unscientific methods on archaeological digs. Barry Marsden quotes, in an article in the *Popular Archaeology* journal, references to Thurnam as departing from his 'pack of asses' in Yorkshire 'to join his relatives at the Wilts County Asylum'. Though he had some 'redeeming qualities', he could be 'stuffy, self-centered, stubborn and long-winded', larding his conversation with 'some of the longest polysyllables the English language has ever been tortured with'. Even so, his writing in twenty-two annual reports, though formal and occasionally high-flown in mid-Victorian style, is clear and reasonably concise, and provides us with much of what we know of life in the Asylum during his period of stewardship.

# 3 - Useful Occupation

The early reports exude confidence and optimism. The importance is emphasised, both by Thurnam and by the Committee of Visitors, of the early transfer from workhouses to the Asylum of anyone 'who may be attacked with symptoms of lunacy, because the prospect of permanent recovery is much facilitated, when the cases brought in are recent'. In the first two years the proportion of recoveries was 'as large or larger than could have been anticipated ...[and]... may be expected still further to increase'. The cases of Eliza Horder and Martha Parsons are early examples:

*    *    *    *    *

*Eliza Horder, an unmarried 'labourer' from Amesbury, was twenty-three when admitted in December 1851. This was her second attack of insanity and had lasted one year. The notes observe; 'Nervous temperament, rolling gait, semi-idiotic countenance ... imperfect articulation of speech ... sullen, childish, cries when not allowed to be with mother, self-willed, taciturn.' Mentally deficient 'more or less' since birth, she was distressed at remaining in the Amesbury Workhouse after her mother was sent to Laverstock Asylum, and made a 'feigned attempt at suicide by putting herself into a water butt ... not deep enough to drown her & placing her legs in first the water did not reach her chin.' Occasionally violent, she was briefly placed with her mother at Laverton, but for the past six months had been at Fisherton House. An early recommendation for discharge was not acted upon, but ensuing monthly entries show that she behaves well at tea parties, 'attends Chapel twice in the day', 'works pretty well and is quite harmless'. On 3 August 1852 she is 'Discharged recovered'.*

*    *    *    *    *

*Martha Parsons, an illiterate domestic servant from Wilton, was admitted on 2 December 1852. It was her first attack. Unmarried, she had had a baby six months before. She is described as cheerful, but excitable and sometimes hysterical, with an impaired memory:*

> *Respectful to superiors, childish, laughing, singing, dancing, crying &c, almost simultaneously ... not dangerous to herself but rather disposed to fight with others ... no signs of Epilepsy or General*

*Paralysis. ... It appears that she some time back formed an acquaintance with a man [named] of very disreputable character who shortly afterwards seduced her, for some time she cohabited with him until she became pregnant and from his previous depraved mode of life of Housebreaking &c, thinking that he might be taken to prison, when about to be confined she thought much on the subject the consequence of which was that about 10 days after her confinement having had a difficult labour, she suffered from puerperal mania and was removed to Fisherton House Asylum where she has been about 1 month.*

*After a fortnight, she appeared 'rather better ... harmless, engages herself in household work &c', but by 26 December she was 'very violent and excited, scalp hot ... Cold affusion of water to the scalp, during this operation she sat quiet, expressing her relief from its effects, subsequently very quiet and composed.' Despite two further minor relapses, she improved to become 'convalescent' by 1 March, and was 'Discharged Recovered' on 22 March.*

*   *   *   *   *

Martha's recovery seems to have been permanent, but Eliza became one of many who would return, as we shall see. Some, it seems, should never have been there in the first place. A woman was discharged in 1852 who had been committed six years previously to Market Lavington Asylum as a 'wandering lunatic' because she refused to give her name, either when found initially near the canal at Trowbridge or during confinement. It turned out that she was a housekeeper from Bath who had walked out on her natural son when he refused to support her. 'The most probable conclusion', reports the Superintendent, 'is that no insanity ever existed'.

In 1855 fifty-eight patients were 'discharged as recovered' compared with 118 admitted, while even those discharged were beginning to return in substantial numbers (nineteen in 1854). It was already apparent that a pattern of growing numbers was becoming established, and that the Asylum faced a future of continual expansion to house a steadily increasing population of the chronic insane. The government's Commissioners in Lunacy acknowledged this as a national trend, urging that 'harmless chronic' pauper patients be sent back from asylums to the workhouses. Thurnam saw no urgency to do this, since he had room for them, and doubted whether the workhouses could provide the 'special attention' which they needed. By the following year, however, overcrowding had become a problem on the female side, and the need to build an extension was agreed. This was the start of a pattern of repetitive piecemeal expansion which was to characterise the Asylum's operation for a century.

Thurnam expressed concern about the conditions under which some patients were brought to the Asylum, often in handcuffs or a strait-waistcoat. On discharge, unsupervised, he feared that some might stop at a pub and suffer an immediate relapse. But he saw no need for financial help on discharge, since 'the majority of the patients are of the labouring agricultural class, and are tolerably secure, on leaving the Asylum, of employment in their respective parishes'.

The patients, as intended, were kept as fully occupied as possible, both as an integral part of their treatment and as a means of keeping down operating costs. Some two-thirds of the 333 patients were 'employed in various ways' in 1856; the farm, kitchen and laundry depended almost entirely on inmate workers, while all of the clothes and shoes were made in-house. A shelter was provided for 'wood cutting and stone breaking in bad weather'. By 1862 the proportion working had slipped back to just over half (fifty-three per cent of the 151 men and fifty-five per cent of the 224 women); in ensuing years, an increasing proportion of those working was employed on 'housework', which meant merely helping to keep the wards clean and tidy. The Commissioners recommended remaking of mattresses as a 'useful occupation for the more imbecile patients now unemployed'.

Entertainment and recreation were also part of the treatment. In 1854 it was reported that patients 'unite in frequent parades with the band of music' and are taken on 'long walks in the country, much to their gratification and advantage'. They might indulge in singing occasionally, but dancing was a different matter; Thurnam felt 'considerable doubt as to the propriety of its formal introduction into asylums for the poor, at least in this part of England. In the asylums of the metropolis, and of Ireland, the case no doubt may be different'. He did not explain why. Evening entertainments were given monthly, while the frequent tea parties were popular. In 1861, 'as usual a large party attended the service at St Mary's Church, on the occasion of the festival of the Wiltshire Friendly Society', and 'a large party of the more orderly and tranquil attended the exhibition of a panorama at Devizes'. Later in the 1860s entertainments seem less frequent; tea parties are held only 'three or four times a year' and musical concerts monthly - but now with dancing, to which Thurnam seems to have been converted.

Generally the local press does not appear to have paid much attention to the Asylum, other than sporadic factual reports of the Committee of Visitors and tender notices for supplies. (There is perhaps an implication here that the Asylum and its inmates did not have a great impact on town life.) An exception occurs in 1863, when the *Devizes Advertiser* reported that one hundred 'Inmates of the Wilts County Asylum' took part in the procession in Devizes to celebrate the marriage of the Prince of Wales.

These celebrations have a link with a patient, George Maton, who was in later years literally to leave his mark on the Asylum for decades to come. Maton's work as an artist in the naive style is well known, and many of his paintings are owned by Marlborough Town Council. The Merchant's House (Marlborough) Trust's *News* of December 1991 records that he 'came from a family of twelve children whose family home was the wedge-shaped building at the junction of New Road and Oxford Street'. He had inherited Huguenot craft skills in coachpainting, signwriting, and furniture decoration.

\*   \*   \*   \*   \*

*George Maton, described as an 'ornamental painter' from Marlborough, was admitted to the Asylum on 28 July 1862, at the age of 44. His disorder is noted as 'monomania of suspicion', which has been preceded four months before by an attack of delirium tremens through drinking, though he has not previously been intemperate. He is said to have 'painted a picture of Savernake Lodge on fire which was ridiculed', and the experience is 'thought to have preyed on his mind'. He is convinced that 'everyone in Marlborough is in league to poison him, and that he is holding communion with the angels by means of the electric telegraph'. He is aggressive and threatening to nurses and attendants, and for some weeks, during which he is visited by friends and by his brother, remains excited and restless, and refuses to work.*

*By the following March he is 'busily engaged in making sketches on the grounds here and painting flags and banners preparatory to the celebration of the Prince of Wales's Wedding Day'. This activity keeps him from writing 'numerous abusive letters to Committee, etc'. Even though his delusions of conpiracy to poison him are as strong as ever, 'his friends are exceedingly anxious to have him out & as they propose to take him from Marlborough he is to-day sent out for three months trial'. George Maton did indeed leave Wiltshire for many years, but he would in due course come back to the Asylum.*

\*   \*   \*   \*   \*

When the chapel in the main Asylum building was being redecorated, as in 1861 and 1866, large parties would walk to Potterne Church and St James's Church, Southbroom, displaying 'most exemplary behaviour'. Normal chapel attendance was about two-thirds of the patient population; in the earliest years it had been three-quarters, but the chapel's capacity of about 250 was and continued to be a limiting factor.

In the 1861 Census, 140 male and 206 female patients are listed. Of only four aged under twenty, the youngest was fourteen. Thurnam, as Enumerator for the institution, annotated seven patients (all female) as 'imbecile' and six (three of each sex) as 'idiot'. Nine were annotated as partially or wholly deaf and/or dumb. Ten male and twelve female attendants are listed and their former occupations given; most of the females had been servants, but among the men are former shoemakers, agricultural labourers and a farm bailiff. The immediate household of John and Frances Thurnam comprised at this time their three children - all boys - a cook, housemaid, nurse, and 'monthly nurse'.

# 4 - Necessity for Enlargement

The 1862 Report, expressing concern at the increasing number of admissions, many of whom 'offer little prospect of restoration to health', looked closely at the trends. The total number of 'Insane Persons, Lunatics, and Idiots' in Wiltshire had increased steadily from 364 in 1847 to 647 in 1861; of this latter figure nearly 300 were being cared for in Workhouses or at home with family or friends. The sixty per cent increase that this represents was compared with a seventy-four per cent increase nationwide. 'In the necessity for enlargement', Thurnam stated, 'this Asylum does but follow on the track of other similar establishments throughout the kingdom'. The national population in asylums had risen from 10,800 in 1849 to 18,022 in 1859.

Since the Asylum opened, on average five or six patients a year had been escaping. Most were at liberty for only a few hours, but if they managed to evade recovery for fourteen days, they were automatically discharged, by law. Thurnam did not 'attach quite so much importance to escapes as some do', and felt that staff vigilance was the answer, rather than bolts and bars which would have been inconsistent with the treatment ethic. He did propose in 1856 the installation of a steam whistle to help forestall escapes, while adding the sensible rider that 'this application of the steam whistle is, of course, only available in an Asylum not in the immediate neighbourhood of a railway station'. Some escapers who were traced within a few days were allowed to remain out for a trial period, as part of the practice of releasing recovering patients on trial before full discharge.

The first suicide was experienced in 1861. The man had jumped out of the window 'during a paroxysm of suicidal melancholia, apparently induced by the consequences of a "strike" among the masons engaged on the Hungerford and Devizes Railway, of whom he was one'.

The inspecting Commissioners in Lunacy regularly commented on the incidence of seclusion of refractory patients (usually in padded cells) and direct physical restraint. From 1857 onwards the occasional patient was locked into gloves and wrist-straps to prevent tampering with a medical dressing. Seclusion gradually assumed an accustomed place in the Asylum's regime, reaching an average of nearly one case a week by 1861. The Commissioners regularly reported also on the incidence of the use of strong canvas clothing to frustrate those who habitually undressed themselves (eg, 'two or three patients of each sex' on their 1862 visit). They would also note the number of beds 'wetted or dirtied' (in 1862, twenty-eight on a typical night) and over several years urged the adoption of a night-watch policy to reduce the incidence, and the consequent need for straw beds.

A few criminal lunatics, typically seven or eight at any one time, were housed at the Asylum. Their crimes, however, appear mainly to have been at the level of larceny or 'stealing an ass', so the apparent lack of any particular security arrangement for them is perhaps not surprising. The term 'criminal lunatic' was shortly to be redefined, after which only one or two so classified were in the Asylum.

A general impression is given, over the course of several years' reports, of a bright place with wards abounding with plants, cages of singing birds and uplifting scripture texts, and cheerful, spacious corridors, but the Commissioners sometimes note exceptions. While always complimentary about the kindness and consideration of the staff towards the inmates, they frequently cite slow progress towards such matters as building extensions, improvements to bare and comfortless refractory wards, more homely furnishings, effective night attendance, and more changes of bath-water. Thurnam, though the Commissioners had the previous year found some of his wards to have a 'bare and monotonous aspect' and some 'especially gloomy', felt able blithely to quote a Dr Paget, 'the Harveian Orator for 1866':

> To my eyes, a Pauper Lunatic Asylum, such as may now be seen in our English counties, with its pleasant grounds, its airy and cleanly wards, its many comforts and wise superintendents provided for those whose lot it is to bear the double burden of poverty and mental derangement, I say this sight is to me the most blessed manifestation of true civilisation which the world can present.

With the number of patients exceeding 450 in 1869, the support systems of the Asylum were showing signs of strain. A new boiler was installed for the 'warming apparatus', new shafts were sunk to enhance the water supply, and the gas works were remodelled and rebuilt. In the preceding few years, following serious complaints from the 'proprietors of adjoining lands' about the sewage from the Asylum, a new water-wheel driven system had been installed, enabling the waste more effectively to be 'distributed over the fields of the Asylum' (by now extended from forty-five to sixty-six acres). As a result, the fields were 'rendered productive to an extraordinary degree', and a dairy was established, making the institution self-sufficient for milk. These money-saving outcomes paid most of the installation costs of the system.

The Asylum was generally being run at a very economical level of cost to the ratepayer. The weekly charge to be paid to the Asylum by the Poor Law Unions in Wiltshire for each of their inmates there was always among the lowest in the country. It remained consistently below ten shillings and was sometimes (particularly when the Asylum was full or overcrowded) below eight shillings. There were hints from time to time by the Commissioners in Lunacy that the charges were set too low, and that a less tight budget would allow improvements to be made more quickly.

The death in 1871 of 'a poor idiot, aged 20, an inmate of nearly eight years' standing', after being attacked by another patient, prompts the questions, how many children were kept in the Asylum, and of what age? Tables in each report show that from time to time children as young as five were admitted as patients, many having had their first attack of insanity at an even earlier age. On average, rather less than one per year aged between five and ten, and another one per year between ten and fifteen, were admitted.

The policy regarding childbirth in the Asylum is indicated only by occasional comments in the Reports. It is stated in 1864 that generally 'when about six weeks old, [the child] is removed to its home or to the Union House, as the case may be'; this seems to take no account of whether or not the mother is fit for discharge. In 1870, 'one of the inmates admitted in March, in a state of pregnancy, was confined of a male child in August. This patient has not yet [ie about December] recovered, and remains in the Asylum'; we are left to wonder, what of the child? We can at least deduce, from the way in which these individual cases appear in annual reports, that they are special and infrequent events.

*     *     *     *     *

*In April 1865, thirteen years after her discharge, Eliza Horder is readmitted at the age of thirty-six. She has had an illegitimate child, now nine years old, and has been 'kept almost entirely by the Parish', in lodgings or the Workhouse. When refused 'leave of absence', or otherwise frustrated, she 'frequently had paroxysms of violence ... threatens suicide, breaks windows &c - has frequently escaped over the walls ... walking about the yard without clothes'. She is 'self-willed and violent', with an 'idiotic expression' and 'unprepossessing' manner.*

*Eliza gives no trouble, working regularly and willingly in the laundry. A year passes with only one cursory entry in the Case Book, but in April 1866 she is noted as 'violent and abusive ... [using] foul language which astonished her attendants' because she was refused discharge 'last Committee Day'. The following month she is recommended for discharge on two months' trial, but Amesbury Workhouse refuses to take her back. She becomes 'excessively surly' and escapes during a tea party, makes her own way to Amesbury Workhouse 'to see her child', but is returned to the Asylum by Salisbury police. From the next note, five months later, we learn that she 'has been more or less troublesome and disorderly' ever since she was brought back'. She has taken to collecting strips of cloth and tying them round herself, for an attempt, it is suspected, either at escape or suicide.*

*After two brief routine entries at six-month intervals, there is a five-year gap. Then, in December 1872 she is 'much as ever ... willful threatening suicide escapes ... She now has a pulsating tumour at the root of the neck'. Six months later the tumour has disappeared; 'Patient is much disgusted at this & maliciously tries to pervert one's remark that one can't feel it any longer into saying that there was nothing the matter. How much pain she felt cannot be judged - her statements could not be trusted'. She is refused an application for discharge on 31 May 1873 and is 'very sullen', but in July suddenly becomes 'exceptionally civil ... making most "natural" inquiries about her son - where he is &c'. This is the prelude to another escape, eluding her attendants 'whilst out for a walk off the premises'. Three days later she is 'brought back by a police man from Upavon unharmed. She did not succeed in getting to her son after all. Of course very abusive.'*

*In November 1885 Eliza, now aged fifty-seven, violent, destructive and using foul and abusive language, attempted 'to throw the contents of her chamber utensil over the Medical Officer and while at Dinner dashed the plates on the floor. Her general health is very indifferent, with signs of a heart problem, and no very strong measures can be taken to cure or improve her. Seclusions being generally tried.' Again this dramatic entry is not followed up, but in March the next year she is transferred to a medical ward 'on account of a large tumour over left breast', which soon becomes 'plainly cystic and the intugement is getting thinner'. A record of her weight at 7st 7lb, in June 1886, is the last Case Book entry for Eliza, but it was not until 7 January 1889 that she eventually died at the Asylum.*

*   *   *   *   *

The inexorable increase in the number of patients was causing major concern. While the numbers of recoveries remained substantial, a pattern had been established that those who had not been discharged as recovered within nine months were likely to stay for many years. The pressure was being felt throughout the country but particularly in Wiltshire, which in the late 1860s had the highest incidence in the country both of paupers (1:12) and of pauper lunatics (1:327); agricultural counties had generally higher rates than industrial ones. Thurnam blamed poverty and drink, at least partially. In many cases, he wrote 'the exciting cause is clearly traceable to intemperance in drink', putting the proportion at twenty per cent of cases admitted from 1867 to 1871, increasing to thirty-four per cent in 1872. He feared that:

Increasing wages, now in many places paid to the agricultural labourer, are of little real advantage to the recipients, but rather to the licensed keepers of public houses, who, profit by the consequent larger expenditure on drink.

He also endorsed a colleague's assessment that the rate of insanity had a close relationship to that of poverty, and quoted another colleague who believed that 'insanity is an upshot of mental inactivity, and our "uneducated cloddish populations" are its chief breeders'. Thurnam stated the problem in forthright terms:

> Part of the increase must be referred to the facilities afforded by recent legislation to the admission of patients, many of whom are sent labouring under slight and transient forms of mental disorder, such as in former days would never have been removed from their homes. Some are brought who ought to be cared for elsewhere, in Workhouses, or even in Prisons. Not a few superannuated and paralytic old people, when they become troublesome in the wards of the Workhouse, are at once removed to the Asylum. In other instances men are brought who should be regarded as offenders against the laws, and punished accordingly. It is an abuse of an Asylum to send to it a man who, maddened by drink, assaults his wife and child, or commits some other vagary or act of violence. It may not be easy in every case to discriminate the excitement of intoxication, acting on a violent temper and coarse nature from mania; but a day or two would generally suffice to decide the question. The journey to the Asylum and the warm bath on arrival often suffice to dispel the excitement; and, it is obvious, that in place of residence in our comfortable wards, there are cases in which a month's discipline at the treadmill would in every respect be the more appropriate treatment.

Thurnam's health had at this time been showing signs of deterioration; he had taken his first holiday in 1867, and was 'absent on account of ill-health' when the Commissioners visited in 1868. The testy and impatient tone present in his reports at this time may have been connected with his illness, or may have been a pent-up reaction to the frustrations of seeing the measure of success attained by his enlightened and benevolent methods swamped and obscured by continual abuse of the system within which they had to operate. In any event, it was to be only a very few years before John Thurnam died, on 24 September 1873. The Commissioners recorded that he had 'endeared himself' to staff and patients, and it was clear to his successor that 'the officers, servants and inmates of the Asylum' had held Thurnam 'in great and universal esteem'.

# 5 - A Monstrous Thing

The tenure of the new Medical Superintendent, Dr James Wilkie Burman, was short but eventful. The Commissioners in Lunacy, noting his 'zeal and ability', pressed him for improvements, and their confidence that he would respond was justified. Though the young Burman had no magic formula to arrest the continuing rise in patient numbers, he was vigorous in pursuing building projects to accommodate them, and improvements in the quality of care.

He discharged nine 'chronic and harmless' patients to their Union workhouses, but warned that there was little more scope in this direction. Not only were the Workhouse facilities unsuitable for such patients, but they were able to do useful work in the Asylum, so their loss would mean paying more staff. Though this policy, spelt out in his Annual Report, was not very different from Thurnam's, Burman made the error of putting the administative advan-

*By permission of WRO*
### Dr James Wilkie Burman

tages before the therapeutical; he received a stern rebuke from Lord Henry Thynne at the Easter Sessions in 1874, as reported in the *Devizes and Wiltshire Gazette* of 9 April 1874. The Warminster Board of Guardians had sought discharge of an inmate, one of their residents and a former servant of the Marquis of Bath, but Burman told them that 'the man's services were required for the farm, and that if they parted with "mild lunatics" they would not be able to carry on their work as they were doing'. Lord Thynne considered it 'a monstrous thing that asylums should be maintained by the parochial authorities, and that sane people should be kept in there simply for the purpose of doing 'farm' work. It was still more monstrous that people of weak intellect should be detained, simply to save the cost of management'. The same meeting of the Sessions discussed a rash of applications for pensions from Asylum staff wishing to leave. Lord Thynne had been advised that this 'was owing to the appointment of a new medical superintendent; and he was not sure that the way in which the new doctor was managing the Asylum was altogether satisfactory'.

Burman increased the staff of attendants and night-nurses, but the increased staff-to-patient ratio, at 1:14, still fell short of the 1:11 average of neighbouring counties. Better night supervision would help meet the Commissioners' complaint that there were still in use seventy-four wooden trough beds, with leaden bottoms and straw mattresses. The infrequency of escapes surprised Burman, considering the 'rather inadequate staff of attendants' and 'lowness of airing court walls'; he perhaps overlooked the store of goodwill and trust which Thurnam had built up. His stated aim to improve the quality of staff, in order to 'develop that more intelligent and humane care, satisfactory and considerate treatment of the insane poor, which the present enlightened age aims for', also seems to show scant respect for Thurnam's well-known aspiration to identical aims.

*   *   *   *   *

*One patient who did escape in Burman's time was Ralph Shewring, a former soldier aged thirty-seven. He was admitted from the Chippenham Workhouse in July 1874, after injuring his wrist with broken glass, showing symptoms of 'General Paralysis' arising from 'religious delusion'. He escaped three weeks later, forcing open the door of an airing court, and explaining after his prompt capture that he 'wanted to get to London to get the Queen to liberate Sir R Tichborne from prison'. [The trial of Roger Tichborne for perjury, ending in his sentence to fourteen years' imprisonment, had received wide press coverage in the early months of that year.] A letter, addressed to Ralph's sister in Bath a month later, by which time he was 'quieter', is attached to his Case Notes.*

*My Dear Sisters and Brothers*
*this is the truth i can not forgive them on my left hand if Jesus Christ*
*was on earth now would you kneel down and Pray to him why not to*
*God and is holy son and holy gohst in heven and obey thy father and*
*Mother and thy Godmother the Queen of England i Would fight for*
*her up to my neck in Blood because i do no she is taking up my part if*
*you comes here to marry i got something to tell you dont fret about me*
*if you do it is sin against the holy Son of God i was born tursday Oct*
*8 1834 at 4 Clock am Who tells me that Why the holy Gohst i should*
*had sent a letter to mary but they told me she was coming here so i*
*must conclude With my best Love to all me Back and head hath had a*
*rough knocking about if you comes here the 23 i will tell you somthing*
*as will make the tears run from your Eyes it is more than a*
*100,000,000 years ago when adam and eve Was made then no man on*
*my Left hand can tell me who sin before Adam.*
    *Shewring Ralph'*
*Nine months later he was 'quite rational and as far as can be ascertained*
*got quit of his delusion', and after a further three months, on 6 September*
*1875, he was discharged.*

*   *   *   *   *

Drug costs had stayed at around £25 to £30 a year throughout Thurnam's time, thus decreasing as a proportion of overall spending. Burman's arrival corresponds, for whatever reason, with an approximate doubling of annual drug spending; it is noticeable also that a small annual purchase of leeches which Thurnam had made is discontinued.

Burman believed in the benefits of 'amusements, recreation and diversion', even if they were 'palliative more than curative', and began to inject new life into the programme. There were frequent regular picnics on Roundway Down and Etchilhampton Hill, and a 'regular weekly entertainment' despite the lack of a special hall. Finding the brass band too expensive, he substituted a piano which, 'played by Miss Greenland, of Devizes, accompanied by the Assistant Medical Officer, on the Piccolo, and the Chief Attendant, on the Bass Fiddle ... provided ample and appropriate music'. There were also magic lantern shows, and a visit in 1875 by the Devizes Hand-bell Ringers. For the chapel services a choir was formed of 'Officers, Servants, and Patients' plus 'kind friends from the town', accompanied by the organist, storekeeper William Nuth. To improve literacy among the patients a night school was started under the same Mr Nuth, a former schoolteacher. Unfortunately the ubiquitous Mr Nuth was dismissed in disgrace the following year. He had been caught sending home items from the Asylum Store to his wife in Devizes, using for the purpose patients who were trusted to go into the town.

Misfortunes, some of them made embarrassingly public, were beginning to afflict the Asylum at a pace which must have been very uncomfortable for Dr Burman. In 1874 a patient accused an Asylum stoker of being the father of her baby. Though the case against him was never proven, he was later dismissed for drunkenness and dereliction of duty.

In the same year an empty coffin was buried 'with the usual religious ceremonies' in the Asylum cemetery, an event which found its way into national newspapers. Burman's explanation why nobody had noticed the absence of a corpse was that the deceased woman had been 'a micro-cephalic idiot of exceedingly small stature and light weight', and the coffin 'much heavier than usual ... being made of fresh and damp elm wood', and containing 'the usual bedding' of sawdust and shavings. The porter, a key figure in the mortuary procedures, was away ill, and nobody else was blamed. Rules were tightened, but there must have been deep embarrassment to Burman and to his masters, the Committee of Visitors.

In March 1875 a male attendant, Ephraim Marsh, was tried for 'unlawfully and maliciously assaulting Charles Little, a lunatic, and inflicting upon him grievous bodily harm'. The *Devizes and Wiltshire Gazette* carried a full report. Marsh did not dispute the evidence that he had been drunk on duty at the time, and had also threatened with violence the constable called to arrest him. The patient, though normally 'melancholy and rarely violent', had had a disturbed and violent week, and had been seen to strike Marsh first. Marsh was convicted, and sentenced to six months' hard labour, with a recommendation to mercy, a sentence which the Commissioners thought too light. They had reason be sensitive to violence in asylums, since one of their number had been killed by a patient at Fisherton House the previous year.

In February 1878, 'a large number of attendants' combined in a 'Round Robin' letter, 'complaining of the quality and quantity of the provisions supplied to them'. The Committee of Visitors found 'no sufficient grounds for complaint', and castigated the leaders for not putting their complaint through the proper channels. As we have seen, there had been rumblings of staff discontent before, with many wanting to leave in Burman's first year, and others were now taking up 'more lucrative posts in other asylums'. Within a month of the Round Robin, the Justices had received Burman's resignation, and he was gone. The Reports do not indicate whether these two events were connected.

# 6 - Not Prisons but Hospitals

Dr Edward Marriott Cooke took over on 19 March 1878, at twenty-six a year younger even than Burman had been on appointment. Cooke ran the Asylum for just over three years, a period in which the number of patients passed both the 550 and 600 levels. In this period, also, new wings for both male and female patients were completed, plus a day-room for entertainments and a special dormitory for suicidal and epileptic patients; a system of 'fire extincteurs' was installed to convey water for firefighting. Though 'a large proportion of box or trough beds' was still in use, 'the old straw mattresses were being done away with, and hair or sea grass substituted'. The Commissioners recommended a new upholsterer's shop,'in which all the hair picking might be done, by old and demented patients now unoccupied'. More than half were now usefully employed, the women largely in the laundry or at needlework and the men on the farm or at various trades, but many of both

By permission of WRO

*Dr Edward Marriott Cooke*

sexes still merely on 'housework'. The chapel was nearly full on most Sundays - Dr Cooke had become the organist and choirmaster - but could now accommodate less than forty-five per cent of the patients.

One readmitted patient in 1878 was clearly not a favourite among the staff:

\*    \*    \*    \*    \*

*A married cloth-worker from Dilton Marsh, Peter Hillman was aged thirty-four when first admitted from Westbury Union in April 1873 suffering from 'mania' arising from 'religious despondency'. His condition was thought to arise from attending many 'prayer meetings for a pouring out of the spirit with his sect all the winter'. He had reached 'an excited state talking most incoherently on religious subjects saying his body was weak in consequence of excessive outpouring of the spirit upon him', and was 'ceaselessly talking day and night', and thus getting no sleep. He is described as having 'a rather long tolerably developed head', 'dark dark eyes', and a 'countenance and manner expressive of melancholy, restlessness and confusion'.*

*After a few turbulent nights, when he tended to strip himself, Peter began to improve, writing 'a calm rational letter to friends', and working regularly on the farm. But within a fortnight he became reluctant to work, and clearly was arousing the intense dislike of the Assistant Medical Officer, who describes him in successive reports as 'a rather exacting fellow' and 'a bit of a prig', then on 21 July we get the following diatribe:*

*He is constantly showing his disposition to lazy self-indulgence & to shirk everything like exertion - at the same time preferring requests for indulgence: sneaks into the water-closet out of sight when it is time to go to the farm ... Stopping his tobacco has had the effect of sending him to work again. Today he was visited by the 'Minister' of his Chapel & showed his dissatisfaction & ingratitude by declaring there was never any need of his being brought here, although the Minister told him he had himself seen him so bad that it was necessary to tie him down to his bed with sheets. Is a marked specimen of a conceited self-satisfied exacting sectarian.*

*But he 'keeps well: probably in his natural state', and the Case Book pages almost breathe the sense of relief in the words 'discharged recovered', ten days later.*

*In less than three years, in January 1876, he was back in the Asylum, with a 'suicidal propensity' brought on by 'religious excitement'. Though he had 'gone on quite well' and been 'sober and steady', Peter had now become 'agitated & queer as before', saying he was a 'very wicked man but no worse than many others'. Though 'despondent and melancholic', and later 'excited' and 'incoherent', he soon showed marked improvement. By May he had progressed from being restricted to exercise in the airing courts*

*to assisting the storekeeper (probably William Nuth, whom we have met),
and at the end of the month was discharged, 'quite recovered'.*

*This time it was under two years before he returned, His 1878 readmission report notes that he has a wife and five children, and that 'at Christmas last [he] had a bad hand & owing to poverty did not get proper nourishment', and consequently 'became low' and susceptible to relapse. In 1879 he walked from Westbury to the Asylum and demanded excitedly to see his brother, who was an inmate; he remained overnight, was restless, noisy and destructive, and was certified insane and readmitted the following morning. Again he recovered sufficiently to be discharged, and worked at odd jobs, but in 1880 he was again readmitted,, hearing 'voices' urging him to commit suicide, which he found difficult to resist.*

*The Case Book carrying further notes on Peter includes entries within the past 100 years, and is therefore still closed. But in later years he was more than once to earn the notoriety of special comment in the Superintendent's Annual Reports, as we shall see.*

*      *      *      *      *

Amusements were reported to be flourishing, with about half the patients attending. A weekly dance and musical entertainment, attended by about 200, would sometimes feature 'Theatrical and Christy Minstrel entertainments' presented 'by the Asylum staff'. Cricket, bowls and other outdoor games were available. But patients in large parties being taken for country walks were 'subject to annoyances from various idlers and loiterers about the lanes and roads where they usually walk'.

Cooke, writing in 1880, found it:

> painful to discover what gross ignorance still exists regarding the treatment received by inmates in public asylums, finding as we do from time to time that there are yet persons who truly believe that 'straight-jackets' [sic] and other objectionable methods of restraint are largely used, and that cruel coercion is still employed in these establishments. This popular error is mainly due to the little opportunity the outside public have of grasping the fact that asylums are not prisons, but hospitals for the insane ... and also to the conduct of those ungrateful patients, who having recovered and been discharged, make complaints as to their wrongful detention or treatment, in order to elicit the sympathy of others and gain their own ends.

Though there is indeed no evidence of 'cruel coercion', some of the treatment practices which Cooke had himself reported the previous year may have seemed harsher to outside observers than to those insiders who were accustomed to them. Seclusion, often in padded cells and demanding the supervision of several attendants, was being used too often for the

Commissioners' liking. They found on their 1879 visit nine women restrained by 'strong sleeves' for one to six weeks, 'for either surgical reasons or to prevent suicide attempts'. 'Recourse to the stomach-pump as a means of introducing food into the system' of patients trying to starve themselves, was 'an unusually frequent necessity'; one woman had been kept alive by 'new milk, eggs, beef-tea, brandy and cod-liver oil being injected twice a day' for three months. An attendant was suspected of having broken the ribs of a patient, while a very violent patient had had to be removed to Fisherton House, which specialised in such cases. Also, a 'young girl subject to epilepsy ... had at the time of her admission from Tisbury Union Workhouse, scars on her arms, the result of wounds, which showed that she had at some time been severely restrained'. Cooke was keen for post mortems to be conducted on all patient deaths, where relatives did not object, both for their scientific value, and also to reveal any injuries 'caused by undue violence', thus 'preventing rough usage of patients in asylums'.

Some of the treatments to calm down dangerously over-excited patients inevitably came to be viewed as forms of punishment. The Commissioners had commented that the fifty-five second duration of the cold shower bath on the male side was 'too continuous', though they seemed satisfied with thirty seconds for the females. In Cooke's time, the Surgery and Dispensary records show, as well as a further doubling of drug costs, the first purchase of water cushions, presumably for use in 'wet-pack' treatment, which was to be an issue in later years.

Only one-third of patients admitted were regarded as curable, and too many were 'old and feeble'. To improve the situation, Cooke wanted admission procedures to include a fuller case history, particularly as to family background, from 'the medical man who certifies as to the patient's insanity'. He felt that a 'Parliamentary Grant of 4s per head', paid to Guardians of Workhouses 'towards the cost of Lunatics maintained *in the Asylum*' had 'promoted the sending of harmless and chronic cases to the Asylum'. He also wanted the government to 'set apart a special place for the confinement of Criminal Lunatics', since their juxtaposition with other lunatics was harmful and difficult to manage.

As far as one can judge from the Reports, Cooke's period in Office seems to have been a more measured and less frenetic one than Burman's. When he resigned in June 1881 to go to the Worcestershire County Asylum (the next stage in a career that would take him to a post as a Commissioner in Lunacy and a knighthood), the Committee of Visitors recorded that they had 'lost an efficient and zealous officer'. Though his successor remarked on the 'admirable condition' in which he found the Asylum, the Commissioners did comment, in Cooke's final year, on the need for more indoor amusement, better floor coverings, and a library, or failing that more books and newspapers on the wards. Furthermore they considered that 'one shirt weekly for day and night use is not enough for the men': in most asylums, it seems, they had two.

# 7 - The Mothers were Less Fortunate

John Ireland Bowes began on 29 June 1881 what was to be a very long period as Medical Superintendent of the Asylum. He was soon faced, as his two predecessors had been, with a succession of suggestions and cajolements from the Commissioners in Lunacy. Their role, after all, was to maintain nationally not only a basic standard but also a continuing improvement, up to the limits tolerable to the justices in each county, advised or pushed by their asylum superintendent. An innovation in one county soon had to be the aim for all. Bowes was able to report that, of measures recently urged by the Commissioners, he had achieved by 1884 better means of fire-escape, enlargement of the laundry, and a new mortuary, but was still unable to provide a detached hospital for contagious diseases, a larger chapel or a recreation hall. Visits to patients remained restricted to two periods of two hours each week, despite the Commissioners' having urged, some years before, an increase to six periods; Bowes's rules specified that:

*Dr John Ireland Bowes*

Visits may not be repeated in ordinary circumstances more frequently than once a fortnight, and it is advisable that letters of inquiry should be confined to the same period. ... A little fruit or cake may be given to a patient; but Visitors are positively prohibited from bringing Wine, Beer or Spirits within the Asylum.

He kept the Commissioners more or less at bay on the topic of recreation and amusement for the patients, holding the Asylum's first athletic sports, watched by 400, in 1882, and in 1889 recording an impressive year's events: twenty-seven dances, five theatrical performances, seven coffee parties, one minstrel and conjuring show, and groups 'sent to three entertainments in town', plus, out of doors, twenty-two cricket and fourteen football matches, dances, and picnics on Roundway Hill. But the Commissioners thought that too few patients were being employed out of doors: Bowes gave several reasons; some were 'too demented and lost to be employed', some were unsafe with tools, some were 'too deluded and dangerous', and some too lazy - a 'common expression' was '"I have not come here to work"', and Bowes had 'no power to enforce submission and compliance'. Many needed inducement even to join the parties taking daily walks, which were 'scarcely appreciated'.

By permission of Pinecraven Ltd

**Asylum Mortuary**

Bowes commented on the 'admirable condition' of the Asylum in his first year, with 'every part ... now more or less brightened by coloured walls, pictures, birds, and flowers', an impression shared in ensuing years by the Commissioners, and by visiting Union Guardians, one of whom wrote in glowing terms about it, as we shall see. But it was certainly possible to get a less uplifting first impression of the place. Bowes's grandson John Leech has described his grandparents' recollections, of 'that first impact of gaunt, grey stone walls, ventilation towers, bare wards, railings, thick grass banks and the impression that even the weeds in the exercise yards had been locked in'.

John Leech, whose father also was Medical Superintendent of the Asylum, lived there for twenty-seven years, and so has a unique vantage-point of its history, which he has recorded in two books, *The Lunatic Years* and *Inside Out*. He describes Bowes at the time of his marriage to Sophie Butlin in 1879, as a 'young, grave, bearded doctor of Kentish farming stock, of little account and less money'. Bowes was aged thirty-one when he came to Wiltshire from the Northamptonshire Asylum, with his wife and first child. 'Wives of Devizes clergy and regimental officers' wives welcomed this new superintendent and, more importantly, his skittish, fun loving wife', as a breath of fresh air after a succession of preoccupied forerunners. He gives a picture of their life in the Asylum:

> The superintendent's rooms were on the first floor of the main block and were no doubt as comfortable as asylum upholstery could make thoroughly institutional apartments. The rooms turned their backs on the barracks and looked out of sash windows on two massive cedar trees and, beyond, to the green fields and hills of Wiltshire. The Asylum rooks did not build their nests in the cedars, nor in the avenue of tall oaks that separated the great spread of the cricket-field from the downward sloping rough grass of the asylum cemetery, but in the tallest trees that cast their shadows over the mortuary and its cinder paths.
>
> John and Sophie were quick to recognise that this thirty year old asylum was a family affair. It had its clerks and a steward, its tailor and gatekeeper, farm bailiff and shoemaker, carpenter and cowman, blacksmith, butcher and baker - perhaps even its candle-stick maker if that had once been the trade of old Snuffy, a male patient in ward Number 3 - or was he in Number 5? On duty in the wards, day and night, were male attendants and female nurses. Only some of these characters carried bunches of keys and whistles and it would be another four years before the male attendants were to be put into uniform - jackets, sleeved waistcoats, regulation trousers and blue cloth caps. Many employees lived outside the grounds and came in each dawn from the villages, but the asylum was a living, self-sufficient world of its own, geared to its six hundred inmates.

A footnote on the matter of attendants' uniforms is that Wiltshire - far from its early Thurnam years in the vanguard of progressive innovation - was the last but one County Asylum in England to introduce them.

The Annual Reports give further indications of the practices regarding childbirth. Over four years up to 1882 four mothers, all patients of a few months' standing, were discharged with their infants. A baby born three weeks after the mother's admission in 1883 was 'handed to the father' after one month, when the mother was 'making fair progress towards recovery'. But in 1889 it is noted that:

> five women were admitted in a state of pregnancy, and subsequently safely confined. The babies all did well, and were in due time removed to their respective fathers, but the mothers were less fortunate, only one recovered her mental faculties, and one remains under treatment, the other three dying from general Paralysis, Phthisis, and exhaustion from maniacal excitement.

The case of Sarah Ann Matthews did not involve childbirth, but does give an indication that it was readily assumed that love could lead to insanity.

*   *   *   *   *

*When Sarah Ann Matthews came to the Asylum from the Cricklade and Wootton Bassett Union in December 1881 she was nineteen. She was a domestic servant, single, and had no children. While living with her parents at Lydiard Tregoz she had two months before developed symptoms of 'mania'. Though 'a well-nourished and healthy looking girl', she had become 'very strange and sometimes violent ... takes little food and seldom sleeps ... constantly knocks her father and mother about ... threatens to drown herself'. She imagined 'that there is always somebody in bed with her at night' and 'hears voices about the room and underneath her bed'. She had 'led a moral and temperate life [with] no domestic trouble or mental anxiety', and no family history of 'Insanity. Epilepsy, Intemperance, Consumption or Cancer'. The 'supposed cause' of her mania is given as 'probably a love affair'. For some weeks she remained 'stubborn and obstinate', refusing to stay in bed at night or to keep her clothes on by day. She 'imagines there is something alive in her bowels', refuses food, and 'has to be fed by force', but by January she was 'greatly improved'. On recommendation for her discharge 'on one month's trial' after a four-month stay, her mother wrote:*

> *I have a comfortable home and can look after my daughter but regard her living I am afraid ... our income will not allow it without the parish will allow something towards supporting her. I was very pleased to hear that she have so far recovered and should be very pleased to have her at home.*

*Parish help was presumably forthcoming, since Sarah wrote from home at Tolly House, Wootton Bassett, during her 'trial' period:*

> *Sir,*
> *Just a line to say that I ham quite as well as can be expected and I hope to continue so and I feel glad to think as I ham as well and all my frends his very glad to think I ham got quite well and out with them as I feel that I had every attention paid to get me well and I ham thankfull I was treated very kind to me while I was under your care and I think that all at Present.*
>
> > *I remain*
> > *Your obedient Servant*
> > *Sarah Ann Matthews*

*Her discharge as recovered was confirmed on 2 June 1882. It is not explained in the case notes why a 'love affair' was supposed to have triggered her attack.*

*   *   *   *   *

Joan Busfield argues in *Men, Women and Madness* that women were susceptible to committal to an asylum, being:

> less likely than men to have alternative means of support and so were more likely to become paupers - a situation in which behaviour considered unacceptable and inappropriate (and consequently 'unreasonable'), such as having an illegitimate child, could well bring them to the attention of the authorities and make a stay in the workhouse or asylum seem like a suitable remedy.

In the Wiltshire Asylum women certainly outnumbered men, but apart from one anecdotal recollection of an alleged case, the available evidence does nothing to support the widely held view that illegitimate motherhood *per se* was a sufficient, let alone a commonplace, reason for committal.

For further reference, we can look at the history of Claybury Mental Hospital, *Claybury, A Century of Caring*, written by Eric H Pryor, who directed the nursing service there. He allows that in its asylum days there may have been 'a small group of admissions' of girls who had been turned out of their homes for fornication, found their way as paupers to the workhouse labour ward, and been certified by the authorities as, perhaps, 'moral imbeciles'. Even if they were sane at the time of conception, melancholia would not be unlikely in such circumstances. Their babies could have been adopted, and a long asylum stay could have ensued. But any such cases, he comments, 'in later years received a disproportionate amount of publicity due to the apparent injustice of their case, and the public liking for scandal'.

# 8 - The Lunatic Artist

Three members of the Highworth and Swindon Board of Guardians made a visit the Asylum in 1886. One of them, William Morris, of Victoria Street, Swindon, wrote about it for a local newspaper. A cutting among the Cunnington scrapbooks held by the Wiltshire Archaeological and Natural History Society provides us with a rare outsider's view in considerable detail:

> The distance from the Green to the Asylum, which is 'just about a mile', as we were told, runs through country roads and lanes, bounded on either hand by hedge-rows, so close that we could almost touch them as we drove along, and forming such a contrast to the road over the Downs which we had just left. The country being flat, the confined hedge-rows prevented our getting more than an occasional glimpse of the Asylum, and then only in portions, until after we had passed the lodge-gates, and we were right in front of the main building. But before we had reached this point our interest in the visit had quickened. The land belonging to the Asylum is 68a.2r.38p. in extent, and is divided between pasture, arable, and shrubbery, the latter mainly bounding the drive between the entrance lodge and the huge gateway, with closed gates, before which we now stood. But, before we had reached this point, it was curious to note various batches of men who were in different parts of the shrubbery and adjacent gardens, and who paused in their work of weeding and cleaning up as we passed along the drive. It was curious and interesting to notice the faces of these men, and to mark their marvellously varying character. They were, of course, from among the more tractable of the patients, and who could be allowed a certain amount of liberty under the eye of a warder. But what a tale they told, and how various. A collection of the races of mankind on the face of the globe could hardly have presented more striking features. There was in particular the morose character: the man who would not condescend to look at you except by a glance from under knitted eye-brows, and with a face as stern and haughty as he could make it. And then there was the face without life, and the eye without fire, and the mind that

was a void, and the stare that was on vacancy: the poor creature who had no place in the living world: who could only wait and be out of it, and who had been brought out into the sunshine on this glorious autumn day, so that his road to his relief might be made as easy as possible.

The party are ushered into the entrance lodge by 'men in a neat uniform', state their credentials as a deputation to visit patients from their Poor Law Union, apparently having given no prior notice, and are taken to meet the Medical Superintendent. They proceed:

> across a large square court-yard, bounded on either side by low one-storied buildings, with a huge chimney or ventilating shaft in the centre, and the entrance proper to the Asylum forming the opposite end of the square. The entrance hall, in which we are now ushered, produces a favourite impression on our first entering it, which is intensified as we afterwards proceed through ward and corridor. The hall is extensive in area, and light and warm in appearance, the ceiling being supported by a number of graceful columns - a place set to catch the sun all day long, and to make the most of it.

Bowes, having given the deputation a 'hearty greeting', expresses his 'pleasure and satisfaction' at their visit. Such visits are 'encouraging to the officers and they are pleasing to the inmates'. The Boards are generally 'very neglectful of an important duty', only two, Salisbury and Bradford, visiting regularly, and the Highworth and Swindon Board not having visited for three years. Morris quotes Bowes as citing religious excitement as the prevailing cause of his inmates' insanity, and as regards Swindon cases, the activities in particular of the Salvation Army which, 'acting on minds naturally weak and easily excited had completely overturned them and left their possessors helpless lunatics'. This startling claim is at odds with the causes given in the contemporary official reports, where heredity and epilepsy are judged as predominant, well ahead of religion and intemperance.

Even making allowance for Morris's by now obvious inclination to dramatic overstatement, it is clear that the interiors are genuinely bright, cheerful, and scrupulously clean and orderly. Tables throughout the wards and corridors are laid out with 'bound volumes of serial publications like *The Illustrated London News, The Graphic*, &c', all in immaculate condition [perhaps because few read them?], plus in the female wards 'flowers, and ferns, and plants in pots'. 'Lace curtains and gay trappings' are at the windows, and the place abounds with 'aviaries, full of singing birds; cages with parrots and cockatoos, pet dogs, a monkey, and a thousand and one other attractions'. Around the walls are 'busts and plaster casts of works of art', and portraits of members of the Royal Family, Gladstone, Disraeli and Lord Shaftesbury. But most remarkably:

> many score of fresco paintings on the walls ... ranging in size from two or three feet up to ten or twenty feet. Some of these paintings may be counted crude, but none of them are rude, while not a few of them display a very creditable amount of artistic ability and really skillful treatment. And then in addition ... over every door ... small wood panels ... on each of which there was painted a shield bearing a coat of arms. ... We were introduced to the artist who had executed all these works - to the lunatic artist of the Asylum. He was a man, apparently, between fifty and sixty years of age, exhibiting to the casual observer no signs of lunacy, yet who had been for 16 years an inmate of the Asylum.

The focal points of interest for Morris and his deputation were the forty-six patients from the Highworth and Swindon Union. They were:

> all tractable under the charge of the officers, although in one partic-ular case the patient was a raving maniac. A religious craze had bereft him of his reason, and although he could recognise some of the deputation, and called them by name, his language was so fearful that it can never be forgotten by those who heard it. Some few others, both men and women, were morose and reserved, but generally the patients not only recognised those of the deputation whom they had previously known, but entered into conversation most readily, and shook hands with them most heartily. As might be expected, there was a general desire for liberty once again, but throughout the whole visit not a word of complaint, or even a murmur, was heard.

The 'lunatic artist of the Asylum' was George Maton, whose second stay in the Asylum had in fact lasted for fourteen years and whose actual age was probably sixty-six at the time of Morris's visit. The Case Books fill in something of his story since his discharge in 1863.

\* \* \* \* \*

*During his nine years away from Wiltshire, Maton had lived in Southampton and London, and had served six months in the Clerkenwell 'house of detention' for a breach of the peace. Early in 1872 he had been 'sent to Colney Hatch [Asylum, London] under Sec of State's order', having had printed and posted up in the streets foul and abusive posters, which insulted the Queen and the 'Bishop of Canterbury' [sic]. On admis-sion he 'was personally so filthy that all his clothes had to be burnt'. He* was brought from Colney to the Wiltshire Asylum, presumably because Marlborough was the parish responsible for his maintenance.

Several pieces of his writing, mostly dated 1872, are attached to his Case Book notes. They are largely rantings about his being poisoned and being held in the Asylum unlawfully. Among addressees of these notes are 'Hon H A Bruce','Mrs Maton of Silverless Street, Marlborough', and 'Thurnham & Co'[sic] (Thurnam was still Superintendent), to whom he concludes, 'If any imps in this place do me an injury I order them to be made into manure'. One note is headed 'The Bloody Bloody Bloody Wiltshire Hell'. The case notes comment, '... of course all the world is wrong and G Maton right.'

There is a long poem in intricate and contorted language, which may be seen as evidence of a highly intelligent but tormented mind. It begins:

> In this Kaanibble Island
> Oh what filthy ways you see,
> In what is call'd a glorious Reign
> Of one that is called She:
> The State and Church and Imps
> Have been a dark rule of three
> In what is call'd this happy Reign
> Of this She that is call'd V.

In all there are sixteen stanzas of similar careful structure, sprinkled with elaborate pun and lavatorial language about what goes into the London water supply, and concluding with:

> The Lee contains excrement
> A River crement is the Lee.
> It next makes a lakeryment
> Then a seacrement at sea;
> Such wretched ignorant ways
> Is unlawful for to he,
> Open your eyes you krankie lot
> Why! pillars of kan you be.

There are no case book entries at all from late 1872 to 1876. (Strange though this may seem, particularly given the acute nature of his symptoms in 1872, it is not untypical of the general pattern found in the Case Books.) Then it is noted, 'Has during the last three years been constantly at work & has been most useful. Remains very insane.' The next entry is in 1878, 'No mental improvement. Is very useful.' After another three year gap, an *abcess on his hip prompts some further entries. The abcess clears up after three months, when, in May 1881, it is noted that he is 'making himself very useful as is his wont in the painter's shop - he has wonderfully improved in condition and appearance ... [but] his mind remains as confused and deluded as ever. ... As a rule he is very tractable and well behaved but at times is subject to violent outbursts of excitement in which he storms, rages and exhibits a threatening attitude - but with firmness always controllable.'*

*The only direct reference to his ward paintings comes in March 1882. He is 'still deluded with the idea that he is in direct communication with the 'Gods' and other spiritual beings. He works in the painter's shop and makes himself a most valuable acquisition to the Asylum, in the way of painting pictures for the various wards'.*

*The Case Book has only cryptic entries from 1883 to 1887, to the effect that his condition is unchanged, and recording his weight quarterly, then states that his subsequent notes are in the Chronic Case Book. This is not available to us, since it remained in use after 1900 and is therefore closed under the 100-year rule. His year of death is given by Marlborough Town Council, however, as 1900. His ward paintings, we are told by an enthusiast for the Asylum's history whom we shall meet later, remained on the walls until they were painted over in 1939.*

Photograph by P Steele

*Graffiti carved on Airing Court walls*

By permission of Pinecraven Ltd

*Campfield – Medical Superintendent's Residence*

# 9 - An Active Generator of Insanity

Bowes's reports continue to indicate year by year the minutiae of asylum life. Beer with the patients' meals is stopped and milk substituted. The vigilance of night-staff is checked by clocks which they must frequently 'peg'. Staff tend to stay in their jobs for many years, but an attendant is poached by another asylum because he is a good cricketer. A large house is built in 1892 for the Superintendent and his family and servants, linked to the main Asylum buildings by a covered walkway; Leech writes that in later years, when the lights came on in this walkway night-staff warned each other by tapping on the radiators that the Superintendent was on his rounds. Visits by Guardians of the workhouses, previously very rare, are gradually built up by steady persuasion to an annual pattern. A few criminal lunatics are still housed. Escapes continue but the frequency is down to one or two a year, and, for the first time, none at all in 1882. A suicide is reported in 1888, the first for twenty years, and only the third since the Asylum opened.

\*　　\*　　\*　　\*　　\*

*Peter Hillman's later career at the Asylum did not help the escape statistics. A pattern was established of his readmission, recovery after a few months and further readmission after decreasing periods, with symptoms more or less the same each time. After two further discharges and readmissions between 1880 and 1882, he escaped on 1 May 1884. Bowes notes in the Annual Report:*

*P.H., when working with the painter, made his escape, and managed to evade the police ... for the statutory period of 14 days, at the expiration of which time he was discharged. He had recovered, and was awaiting his discharge, but was too impatient to wait a few days for his legal removal.*

*In 1885 he was back in the Asylum, and in 1887 again made an escape which provoked the Superintendent to make a testy comment in his Annual Report:*

*Two men made their escape together during the night of the 20th May;*

*one was recaptured at once, but the other [ie Peter] (an experienced hand at getting away) managed to hide himself for the statutory period of 14 days, and at the expiration of this time, had the audacity to write, advising a female patient to escape and offering her marriage.*

*There is no mention of his wife, who had still been alive and apparently loyal up to at least October 1880.*

*His story continues with a readmission in June 1888, his fiftieth year. The Board of Guardians for Westbury and Whorwellsdown, visiting on 15 November the same year, report that they consider him to be a promising case for possible discharge, but he appears to have remained a patient at the Asylum until his death on 26 February 1890.*

*   *   *   *   *

Seclusion was still practised, and was not discouraged by the Commissioners, though it was losing favour in many asylums. Bowes thought it 'more calming and humane than a resort to manual restraint, which is at best irritating to the patient': physical restraint was still used only as a medical aid. The practice of wet-packing, however, was being used up to a dozen times a year as, Bowes insisted, a skin treatment:

> In the insane this important membrane is invariably found defective, either dry like parchment and inactive, as observed in melancholics, or greasy and clogged, as found in maniacs. ... In the absence of [Turkish] baths here wet pack is used as a substitute, and though beneficial (and recoveries can be traced to its use) it partakes too much of the form of a restraint, and is apt to be looked upon as a mild form of punishment.

The wet-pack was classified by the Commissioners unequivocally as a form of restraint, but they raised no objection to its use until 1895. It was then banned 'by reason of an unfortunate occurrence attending its application in a different form in another Asylum'. Bowes still considered it 'rational, humane, and beneficial', and continued to use it occasionally, though with 'a nurse continually present'.

Bowes reported in 1886:

> The Asylum has received a second visit from a man named H.W., who can probably boast of being the greatest malingerer in the 'insane world'. On his former visit, he was classed as insane and was evidently so favourably impressed by the kindness he received, as to lead him to note the institution as worthy of a second visit. This time he was less fortunate, and expressed himself as disappointed, and in consequence threatened never to favour

Wiltshire with his presence again. This man has been, and generally more than once, in the majority of English Asylums, and also in those over the border. He has too, been in similar institutions in America, and resided for various terms in the prisons of that and this country. His notoriety sometime since led to a resume of his career being recorded in a leading article in a London daily paper.

The addition of a new storey in 1889-90, which had been provided for in the original design of the building, staved off the overcrowding problem for only a very few years. A scathing report by the Commissioners in 1895 charged that the Committee of Visitors (since 1889 a Committee of the new Wiltshire County Council) 'in omitting to adopt measures for relieving [overcrowding], have failed in their duty to the unfortunate patients committed to their charge'. Bowes responded that the Commissioners had inspected on a wet day, when things were likely to be at their worst; he felt that 'a want of mutual confidence [was] inspired by surprise visits paid at long and uncertain intervals'. By the following year improvements, already in hand in 1895, had provided places for 125 more patients, and ensuing reports by the Commissioners were complimentary, including one of 'unstinting praise'.

On his arrival at the Asylum, Bowes had assessed that only forty of the 613 patients were curable, and the rise above 700 in 1893 and 800 in 1897 was not unexpected. The reasons for the rising trend, which was common to all public asylums, were debated both nationally and locally. Bowes saw 'no reason to think insanity is increasing in this County'. Though there had been a rise in the numbers of lunatics in Wiltshire from 665 in 1861 to a peak of 958 in 1881, from then the number decreased to 913 in 1891 - and proportionally, down from highest in the country before 1870 to fifth highest in 1891. The incidence was higher in agricultural than industrial counties; 'low wages and deficient food', Bowes considered, were 'an active generator of insanity in agricultural districts'. But the Asylum Chaplain stated what seemed to be the popular view, that due to moral and social causes, and 'rushed' lives, 'this terrible malady is gaining ground in our midst'. Even Bowes conceded that 'the disposition in these days of hard competition and doing everything in a rush, working seven days a week, and turning night into day, is telling its tale'.

Over the course of a few decades the asylums had developed into what Andrew Scull calls 'a convenient and culturally legitimate alternative to coping with "intolerable" individuals within the family'. Because there was no clear demarcation between the sane and the insane person, and because the asylum practitioners believed fervently in the efficacy of their treatment, there developed 'an ever-wider practical application of the term "mental illness"'. The incidence of lunacy was indeed increasing, Scull argues, but only because its definition was widening, not because there was a 'slow epidemic of schizophrenia', as some have claimed.

What was unarguable was the increasing trend in the proportion of the County's lunatics housed in the Asylum as compared to those looked after elsewhere - in the workhouses or with relations or friends. It rose from fifty-eight per cent in 1877 to seventy-four per cent in 1891; Bowes quotes government statistics confirming this as a national trend, and writes, one hopes tongue in cheek:

> The collection of so many in Asylums is alarming to the public, and leads to the belief that insanity is on the increase, so much so that a pessimist prognosticates that in years to come the insane will out-number the sane, that the country will be in the hands of the former, who will confine the few sane persons in Asylums.

He blames the Government allowance of four shillings a week to workhouses for each of their patients in the county asylum for:

> concentrating lunatics in Asylums, particularly the 'village fools', who were formerly the terror and fun of the neighbourhood in which they resided, and who are now disappearing from public view. ... In some cases, too, patients sent to the Asylum suffering from extreme physical weakness and emaciation find it preferable to be classed as lunatics and to enjoy the comforts of an Asylum life, even if they have to feign insanity for the purpose, rather than face the privation and destitution outside, where a man frequently has to maintain himself and keep his wife and family (paying rent and club money) on 10s a-week. Insanity must be the natural outcome of such evils.

No distinction between mental handicap and mental illness had been established until the mid-nineteenth century. Had such a distinction been recognised before the 1845 Act, the history of the pauper asylums may have been a happier one, since different kinds of provision could have been made. Most 'discharged recovered' cases were in the realm of acute mental illness, while it was the 'chronic harmless' mental handicap cases which were unlikely to recover. Since the workhouses were reluctant to house them, particularly once the government rewarded that attitude, these cases swamped the system. The distinction was not legally recognised until 1886, when the Idiots Act allowed local authorities to provide special asylums for 'idiots' and 'imbeciles', but without compulsion there was little response. The Wiltshire Committee of Visitors received in 1893 an approach to join Hampshire, Dorset and the Isle of Wight 'for the provision of a joint Asylum for the reception of idiot children', but they 'saw no need for the erection of any such Building so far at any rate as this County was concerned, and [were] not prepared to co-operate in any such scheme'. Though they did not change the Asylum's role that year, they did change its title; it was no longer to be 'The Asylum for the Insane Poor in the County of Wilts', but 'The Wilts County Asylum'.

Several specific cases are noted of patients inappropriately sent to or retained in the Asylum. The Commissioners criticise the presence, working in the tailor's shop, of 'a little boy, C.P., ... who looked bright and intelligent', while:

> One, aged 8, is an idiot subject to epilepsy, perfectly harmless, but requiring some attention and nursing, and now it is feared doomed to spend the remainder of his life in an asylum, where ... he will be sure to imbibe the depraved habits of his associates.

Melksham workhouse refuses to accept the return a ten-year-old girl because she is 'restless and noisy, uses bad language, and is quite unable to learn'. The Committee of Visitors complains that workhouses send to the Asylum 'almost moribund' patients, who 'often die within a few days'. Bowes considers that the re-certifying of such cases should require independent medical opinion, and not rest solely with the Medical Officer of the workhouse; 'the Officers connected with Workhouses must expect to have troublesome cases to deal with'.

*     *     *     *     *

*One troublesome case which had been referred by Malmesbury Union in 1884 was Lucy Beard. She was a single domestic servant aged 21, from Eastcourt Crudwell. The Supposed Cause of her attack was given as Hereditary, and her Family History as 'Mother very strange in her mind, Brother an Imbecile & two Uncles in an Asylum, also an Aunt Baily in this Asylum'. Though there was no background of domestic trouble or mental anxiety and she had not been addicted to drink, it was noted that she had 'Not led a moral life of late'.*

*The local doctor compiling the Medical Certificate had written, 'When she goes out she dresses in a grotesque fashion altogether unsuitable to her station in life. Although she converses rationally on many subjects she does not seem to recognise her poor position in life. She tells me she wants to go to Balls & dances and wants horses to go out riding on and that the Baker's cart which she mounted the other day and from which she was with difficulty ejected was not half good enough for her & she ought to have a carriage.' Her mother is unable to keep her indoors; she dresses up 'in a fine ridiculous way', goes out to the nearby villages and 'stops out with men sometimes nearly all night'. She gets violent and threatens suicide when her father keeps her in. 'Mr Smith, Rector of the Parish, tells me that her behaviour is so strange that she is becoming a shame and scandal to the neighbourhood. She asked him when being brought to see me if he would take her out hunting next day.'*

*Regular Case Book entries for four years, until January 1888, show little change. Lucy is often 'troublesome and abusive', though usually 'tractable', and her physical health is good. Then suddenly the tone changes; the next entry, in June 1888, reads 'Apparently recovered, is to be discharged on trial, for the last four months has been quite tractable & well behaved, occupying herself & behaving in a perfectly normal manner'. At the end of her trial period, on 18 July 1888, she is 'Discharged Recovered', and does not appear to have returned to the Asylum in later years.*

\*     \*     \*     \*     \*

*Less fortunate than Lucy was Jane Hubbard, in that she was still a patient for at least eleven years, and probably a lot longer, since her records are continued beyond 1895 in a Chronic Case Book which is closed under the 100-year rule. A 38-year-old single domestic servant from Alderbury, she had been admitted suffering from 'religious delusions. She had been 'restless and somewhat depressed and desponding [sic] - is under the delusion that she sees "The Spirit" by night and believes that she can feel it walking upon her'. Apart from a brief period early in her stay when she temporarily 'seems to have got rid of her delusion', the Case Book records no improvement and no change. An unusual feature of her case notes is a copy of a letter, with no associated comment and no record of a reply. It is headed Tonbridge, Kent, dated 1 March 1884, and reads:*

*Dear Sir*
*I should be much obliged if you will favour me with a few lines regarding* Jane Hubbard*, who was forwarded to you from the Alderbury Union on the 20th Feby. The poor woman has worried me for more than two years with her eccentricities, & the gentleman whom she is 'divinely appointed to marry' is an intimate friend of our family. Her unseemly overtures to him, have been the cause of much annoyance. I am desirous to know if you think her case admitting of any hope of cure. Her parents say she had water on the brain at 20 years of age, & has been strange at times ever since. There has never been any charge of immorality that I am aware of against her - but her persecution by letters and in personal solicitations of the gentleman I refer to have been very painful. It would be a great satisfaction to know what you think of her.*
    *Believe me*
        *Faithfully yours*
        *Mary Whitehead.*

\*     \*     \*     \*     \*

Early diagnosis was a recognised enhancement to the chances of curing acute cases, but a strong body of legal opinion existed which considered that this involved a committal process which was too informal, and thus carried a danger of 'unjust confinement on the grounds of derangement'. An argument had raged for forty-five years about whether a magistrate should be involved in the certification proceedings. Lord Shaftesbury, presiding over the Lunacy Commission, consistently and vehemently opposed this, believing that formalisation of the process would delay the start of treatment so that many potential cures would be lost, and the asylums would in time receive only the most hopeless or the most violent cases. Five years after his death the measure which he had opposed even to the brink of resignation was incorporated in the Lunacy (Consolidation) Act, 1890. Predictably, it contained a mass of legal requirements aimed at safeguarding the rights of patients and potential patients. Brian Watkin, in his detailed review of *Documents on Health and Social Services, 1834 to the Present Day*, observes that:

> Not surprisingly, with all this legal apparatus, doctors came to consider admission to an asylum as the last resort in the treatment of mental illness. Both mental nurses and doctors who wished to specialise in psychiatry found that matters of law and procedure figured as prominently in their training as did the causes and treatment of mental illness. Together with the tendency to build very much larger mental hospitals at this time, the Lunacy Act has been held responsible for the era of custodial care which succeeded much of what was hopeful and forward-looking in British psychiatry in the mid-nineteenth century.

A widespread feeling that the incidence of insanity was still increasing was refuted in 1897 by a special investigation by the Commissioners in Lunacy. Local statistics were in line with their finding. As to the causes of insanity, Bowes had written in 1896:

> There is a want of evidence that intemperance in drink causes much personal and direct insanity in this County, but the evils of parental intemperance are marked, and the cases arising therefrom more numerous. ... Moral depravity, which exists to a great and unknown extent in rural districts, is an active generator of insanity, and it is a sad sight to see the lives of young people and persons in the prime of life wrecked by such excesses.

Over the next few years, however, drink, in-breeding in agricultural communities, and rapid industrialisation were variously claimed as contributory factors.

*By permission of Pamela Colman*

*Porter's Lodge Entrance*

# 10 - Apart from Curiosity

Schemes to provide for the harmless chronic insane outside asylum confines were proposed both locally and nationally. One was promulgated in 1900 by G P Fuller, a member of Wiltshire's Visiting Committee, to equip spare wards in selected workhouses for such patients. He provided costings which claimed that the workhouses, despite the loss of the four shillings per day government subsidy for sending an inmate to the Asylum, would still make a small saving on such a scheme. But his proposal was overtaken by two government programmes.

Though proposals from the Royal Commission on the Feeble-minded and Poor Law, intended to relieve asylums, were awaited with little confidence, a scheme was developed under earlier Poor Law legislation 'for the combination of Unions for the institutional care of the feeble-minded'. By 1912 nine Unions in Wiltshire had combined to purchase a site adjacent to the Asylum, but it would cater only for cases already dealt with by the workhouses and was 'not expected to afford much relief to the Asylum'. To help ease the overcrowding, twenty 'harmless' patients were discharged to workhouses in 1906, and for the first time in over thirty years, patients were 'boarded-out', fifteen being sent in 1907 to Dorset County Asylum and more in subsequent years.

Measures such as these helped to hold the number of patients in the Asylum at around 980 from 1903 to 1910. A larger factor in this stability was a steady fall in the number of admissions, though this was counteracted by an unusually low death rate in these years. By 1912, however, the old upward pattern had reasserted itself. Patient numbers surged above 1000, prompting urgent plans for a new detached block for 200 patients; the cost was estimated at £27,000, more than the original cost of the whole Asylum sixty years before.

Bowes noted in 1905 that 'the system of treatment remains much upon the usual lines', and his comments the following year might equally well have been written in the 1860s:

> Though recovery in the majority may be hopeless, there is always some improvement to be instilled by such means as amusements and bright surroundings, aided by well-trained, experienced and sympathetic Attendants and Nurses to comfort the distressed and rouse and direct the afflicted to healthier interest in themselves and to improvement generally.

Though the treatments had not changed, the ratio of attendants and nurses to patients had steadily improved, with substantial benefits to the lives of patients. Comparing the five years 1881-86 with 1901-06, while average patient numbers had increased from 620 to 963, there was now one attendant for every nine patients, whereas there had been only one for every thirteen. This allowed much closer attention to the needs of each patient, with the result that the number restrained had reduced from forty-eight to sixteen, those secluded from 258 to twenty, and the number of deaths requiring an inquest from fourteen to only one. Escapes over the five year period had fallen from thirteen to eight; where an escape was found to have resulted from an attendant's lack of vigilance, he was liable to be 'called upon to pay the expenses attending the recapture'. A suicide in 1908 was the first in the Asylum for twenty-four years. It was noted also that by 1904 'the use of narcotics in the shape of sleeping draughts has almost been abolished'.

Patients leaving the Asylum for temporary trial periods were also better provided for, receiving from 1899 a monetary allowance if their relatives' means were 'inadequate to provide the necessary sustenance to complete recovery'. This had been authorised under the Lunacy Act of 1890, but Wiltshire had needed some nudging from the Commissioners before responding.

The pattern of frequent discharges and readmissions, exemplified by the case of Peter Hillman some years before, seems to have continued. Of 165 patients admitted in 1899, twenty-one had been in the Asylum before. Of these, eleven had been patients more than once, one of them as many as six times. Sixty-four patients were 'Discharged Recovered' in the same year; of these forty had been in the Asylum less than a year and another thirteen between one and two years. The pattern was clear, as it had been for many years; if you failed to get out quickly you were unlikely to get out at all.

The Commissioners (now including Dr Marriott Cooke among their number), though generally not unduly critical, still felt the need to urge more provision for the useful employment of patients, with only forty-six per cent in 'any useful occupation', a new chapel to allow improvement in the 'very low percentage' attending Sunday services, and closer attention to the needs of child inmates. Children under ten were still being admitted, and in 1907 the Commissioners suggested the transfer of 'two little boys' from the male to the female side.

The Boards of Guardians of most of the county's workhouse unions were by this time making annual visits to inspect the premises and their own patients. Among their names is found Dr James Wilkie Burman, returning quietly to visit the Asylum as a member of the Hungerford and Ramsbury Union deputation, thirty-two years after his resignation as Superintendent. The Guardians' reports are generally favourable and bland: the wards are 'bright, airy, cheerful', everything is kept 'beautifully' amid 'warmth and apparent enjoyment'. To the Bradford Board, visiting in 1905, the scene is idyllic:

> Passing from place to place we went through a number of court-yards or enclosures, where large numbers of the inmates were enjoying themselves in their various ways, playing games &c. Everyone seemed to be doing just what pleased their individual fancy, and such a large amount of freedom within the boundaries of the Asylum made it difficult for an outsider to discover where the element of restraint came in.

Such reports may not be surprising considering the substantial income the Boards were receiving for each patient from their area in the Asylum. Even so, one Board was not averse to characterising the visitors' waiting room as 'small, dark and cheerless' with no fire, while others found the Chapel - still the original one within the main building - 'a dull, unsightly place and altogether inadequate', which had 'the appearance of a paupers' chapel indeed'.

The attitude of the general public towards the Asylum was mixed. Bowes complained in 1901 that 'unfortunately little interest apart from curiosity is taken by the public in the Asylum', and issued a plea for the donation of 'surplus books and illustrated papers'. But among the world outside there were numerous benefactors; Lord Edmond Fitzmaurice, for example, was a regular donator of flowers for the wards, while Mrs Bayfield Clark of Wingfield would send a Christmas letter to every patient.

Though the entertainment programme was not very well attended - figures of twenty-two and twenty-eight per cent are reported - it did have its highlights, such as the visit by the Devizes Musical Association in 1902 to perform *Snow White*. A clue to the lack of enthusiasm may lie in the high-minded nature of the programme. 'These are thoroughly social evenings which, in necessitating moral restraint and rousing the patients without exciting them are most curative and beneficial'. The number attracted by the new 'Band of Sacred Music with Songs on Sunday evenings' is not stated.

A new Chaplain, Canon H H Kilburn, seems to have injected new dynamism to the Asylum's spiritual life. Appointed in 1908, having already had 'successful experience of Asylum work', he reported at great length on his activities. He had, for example, 'catechised the patients to ascertain how much they remembered and understood of the last sermon'. Whether this approach tended to increase or decrease chapel attendance will never be known, since the Canon sadly died after only seventeen months in office. He was commended for his 'broadmindedness and genial manner' and for the 'great impression' he had made. Kilburn's successor tried hard to follow his act, drawing 231 patients to a Lantern Service on 'The Passion', which was not repeated because 'it was considered not quite suitable for the patients', and reporting that he had visited the Asylum 539 times in 1912.

It was in January 1914 that John Ireland Bowes retired after thirty-two years as Medical Superintendent. He had presided over a period during which, the optimism of the era of Thurnam and his contemporaries having evaporated, the overriding need was the mere containment of an apparently ever-increasing tide of the insane. His successor, Dr Sydney John Cole, who had been Bowes's deputy since arriving at the Asylum in 1902, assesses Bowes as very much the autocrat, who had 'forgotten much of his knowledge of general medicine and failed to keep up with its advances', but concentrated on the administrative side, where 'he showed marked ability and assiduity. He was a good disciplinarian, kind, always eager to promote the comfort of his patients and staff.' Compared with Cole's previous asylum at Colney Hatch:

> The Officers and staff took greater personal interest in the patients
> ... the atmosphere was less rigidly institutional, a little more home-
> like. ... For that, we had chiefly to thank Bowes and his diplomacy.
> Also, the officers at Devizes were generally on excellent terms with
> one another; there was little of the quarrelling so common in the
> London County. For that happy state of things Bowes deserves
> very much of the credit.

A pointer to Bowes's relationship with his patients is given by a comment registered by the Guardians of Trowbridge and Melksham Union following one of their visits. The patients 'seemed to regard Dr Bowes as he passed them quite as their friend, and it was surprising what control he exercised over them by his presence and looks'.

Bowes's salary, at £1000 in his later years, was five times that of Cole who, as his deputy, had been paid only the same salary as the Asylum clerk. There was apparently no policy to nurture the deputy to succeed to the Medical Superintendent post, and Cole had clearly made no assumption that he would do so, since he had applied and been shortlisted for the equivalent post at four other asylums in the previous few years. This may account, at least in part, for the rather distant relationship which is suggested by Cole's comments on Bowes.

# 11 - Subjects to be Dealt With

Cole very soon was earning every penny of his greatly increased salary, with the problems brought by the outbreak of war. He had to look after more patients, with fewer staff and without the benefits of building projects which had been started but could not be completed. Ninety patients came from the Bristol Asylum at Fishponds when it was taken over by the War Office in 1914, two Belgian refugees were received from Colney Hatch, and later in the war 200 came when the US Army took over the Portsmouth Borough Asylum. The number of patients peaked at 1131. By 1915 Cole was left without Assistant Medical Officers, both Drs Leech and MacPhail being on active service, and had to manage with two local 'medical gentlemen ... acting efficiently as locum tenens'; sixty-nine employees in all were serving in France by 1917 and among these, inevitably, were several casualties.

*By permission of John Leech*
### Dr Sydney John Cole

With overcrowding and lowered standards of care inevitable, serious health problems arose and the death rate doubled, in 1916 exceeding twenty per cent of the average daily number resident. The main causes were pulmonary tuberculosis (then known as phthisis) and dysentery, 'two diseases specially fostered by overcrowding'. Contributory causes were thought to be the lack of open-air treatment for tuberculosis, and the self-rationing of meat, flour and sugar that had been requested by the national Food Controller. It had not been realised how much the 'very liberal diet previously provided' was in fact a necessity, and that mental patients probably 'actually required more food than ordinary persons'. Though the overcrowding was abated 'largely through the operation of these diseases which it has itself provoked', the death rate was 'not likely to subside speedily to its former level', and indeed did remain high, as in many other asylums, until well after the war was over.

The war did not 'appear to have led to any increase of lunacy in Wiltshire', Cole reported in 1915:

> There appears rather to have been a decrease, in spite of the apparent increase of population by influx of soldiers, labourers, etc, from other parts of the kingdom to the great camps of Salisbury Plain. ... The decrease in fresh admisssions ... is even more marked in females than in males.

This trend was still present the following year, despite the further complication of the first psychological victims of the war. Of six soldiers admitted, 'in four of them wounds or stress of campaign may have played some part in the causation of the anxiety', while among civilians:

> The cases in which Mental Stress is entered as a factor include seven men reported to have suffered from war anxiety, either from the prospect of compulsory military service, or on account of sons in the army, or other circumstances arising out of the war, and no less than fifteen women who were stated to have worried about loved ones absent on military service, ... [but] the total incidence of mental stress as a factor ... is relatively a little less than in the previous year, besides having been occasionally exceeded in recent years before the war.

The return of the evacuated patients in 1919 to Bristol and Portsmouth reduced the patient population to 891, a level well below that of the immediate pre-war years. But the lower numbers brought new problems. The maintenance rate per patient, charged to their parenting Boards of Guardians, had already begun to rise due to some financial mismanagement and the exigencies of the war; now, with fewer patients among whom to share the *per capita* costs, and with the interrupted building contracts having to be reinstated, the rate, normally around or below ten shillings per week, rose rapidly year by year. Exacerbated by post-war Union demands for higher staff pay and shorter hours, it reached a peak of twenty-eight shillings before beginning to fall back in 1921. But the staff were reported generally to have been co-operative, and even at this level the rate was well below the national average.

To outward appearances, the theme of the early post-war years was to re-establish the practices and standards of the decades before 1914. There was no great difference in patients' lives or in the general routine of the Asylum, devoted as it had become to no better than containment of the apparently insoluble lunacy problem. Little in the way of practical change seems to have been experienced from the Mental Deficiency Act of 1913, which defined certain grades of mental defectives as 'subjects to be dealt with', which usually meant being committed to an institution, and set up a Board of Control to replace the Lunacy Commissioners. But some of the traumatic experiences of the war had placed new demands on the science of psychiatry, and arising from these, new ideas and developments in treatment, which were to have a marked effect on Asylum life in years to come.

In 1919 Cole, together with his deputy Dr John Leech, newly returned from war service in the RAMC, attended a course 'studying war neuroses' at Ashhurst Neurological War Hospital, Oxford. There, Cole wrote, 'the very latest methods of treatment of mental diseases have been practised with extraordinary success'. He hoped that the law might be 'amended to allow the treatment of incipient mental diseases without the necessity of certification'. The methods studied by Cole and Leech might have included those of two neurologists of that time, described by Pat Barker in her 1991 novel *Regeneration*, which she based on their own factual accounts of their work. She contrasts a graphic and horrifying account of the harshly applied use of electric shock treatment by Dr Lewis Yealland with the more sympathetic methods of Dr W H R Rivers. Admissions of servicemen or ex-servicemen, begun, as we have seen, in 1916, are recorded until 1923, at a rate of from twelve to twenty-one per year, without specification of the causes.

Though Cole and Leech were no doubt better informed about the new treatments than before, no move is evident on their part to introduce them at this time. The old routine predominated, and even by 1926, reliance was 'being placed on the tactful handling of the patients, natural sleep, and in suitable cases the prolonged bath'. The latter, apparently the only innovation, was a calming procedure which succeeded the wet-pack treatment. Patients would stay in the bath under continuous observation for up to seven hours, with a constant temperature and water level being maintained, and with a sheet and board over the bath to enable meals and drinks to be taken. In 1922, if little else was changing, there was another new name, the 'Asylum' title was dropped and replaced with 'Wiltshire County Mental Hospital'.

Cole was preoccupied by the more mundane but increasingly urgent problems of hygiene and sanitation. TB and dysentery, introduced by the wartime overcrowding, proved difficult to eradicate. It does seem surprising that, twenty years into the twentieth century, the Commissioners needed to comment:

> We think that proper toilet paper should replace the rather casual supply of newspaper in the WCs, and that a washbasin should be placed in each sanitary annexe where no such convenience is close at hand.

By 1922 they could report more favourably on personal hygiene matters, but still felt the need to push for further improvement:

> So far as possible, care is taken to see that patients wash their hands on all proper occasions, toilet paper is provided for use in the w.c.'s, and every endeavour is still made to induce the more sensible patients to use toothbrushes. ... [But] none of the male patients are shaved, and those who desire to be have to resort to the use of pumice stone.

The death rate among patients had fallen dramatically since the disastrously high wartime figures; by 1919 it was down to pre-war levels at eleven per cent, and by 1923 as low as six point five per cent, well below the national average for public mental hospitals. Nevertheless, dysentery and TB continued at high levels right through the 1920s, causing several deaths each year. The Hospital escaped the influenza epidemic of 1921, when it was 'rife in the district' as well as nationally, but was badly affected by the disease in 1923, in 1926 when seventeen per cent of patients and staff were affected, and in 1930 when it caused the deaths of numerous 'aged or debilitated patients'. By 1930 a pathological laboratory was an agreed necessity to combat diseases, while the Hospital's sanitary arrangements were still considered to be 'dangerously out of date'.

Reports of this period by the Board of Control Commissioners (no longer 'Commissioners in Lunacy') made many sharp criticisms. In 1927 they observed 'rather more noise among the more troublesome male patients than among the females of that class', and also 'a lack of ornaments, plants, flowers, and such like' in some wards, and day rooms appearing 'very bare and comfortless'. Flowers were lacking, some bird cages were empty, and there were lapses in cleanliness and routine maintenance. Their 1929 report complains of inadequate provision of books, literature and hand towels, and of 'five children under the age of 16, mental defectives', who should be housed elsewhere. The number of patients put in seclusion, having been low for some years, had jumped to sixty-five. The Commissioners rarely failed, however, to praise the standard of medical and nursing care.

The general lack of enthusiasm and dynamism at the Hospital implied by the Commissioners is apparent in the Medical Superintendent's reports of the time, which are short, routine and stereotyped. But occasionally an aside comment opens a window on Hospital life:

- A woman died after fifty-six years as a patient, and a man after forty-nine years.
- The 'Service' patients, in the view of the Ministry of Pensions inspector, 'appear to be well cared for, and to be receiving the privileges of their class'.
- An 'operating chamber for a cinematograph for the recreation hall' was being built.
- New aluminium plates, basins and mugs seemed in 1922 'to answer their purpose well', but two years later the old earthenware ones were reinstated.
- The proportion of all recoveries to all admissions in 1928 was a mere twenty-five per cent.
- An accident to a patient was reported which involved 'the swallowing of half-a-crown whilst imitating a conjurer'. X-rays did not locate it.
- A few escapes continue to be reported each year, rarely more than five or less than two.
- The reports of a suicide in 1924 and two in 1929 confirm that the consistently low rate was being maintained.

Patient numbers had risen further, though for new reasons. The new block on which work had been suspended during the war was completed in 1924, but there were insufficient patients for it to be operated efficiently. Consequently, seventy females were brought in from Middlesex and forty males from Berkshire. The former peak of 1131 was exceeded in 1925, and the number stabilised at just above that level for several years. As far as Wiltshire patients were concerned, the number was rising at an average of twenty per year.

Difficulties were being experienced in maintaining the professionalism of the nursing staff. Before the war twenty per cent of the males and five per cent of the female nurses had held the certificate of the Medico-Psychological Association. Post-war, the proportion af qualified males was rising (to twenty-eight per cent by 1927), but that of the women was falling. Only seven women were reported as qualified in 1926 and none at all the following year. Also nursing staff ratios were lower than elsewhere. In response to the urging of the Commissioners for an improvement, the Visiting Committee noted how difficult it was to engage female career nurses, but in 1927 were able to appoint a Sister-Tutor. In the same year a new residential block was completed and occupied by a sister and thirty-two female nurses.

*By permission of WRO*

Recreation Hall

# 12 - To Lessen the Stigma

The Mental Treatment Act of 1930 made what Brian Watkin has described as 'the first real breach in the legal fortress erected by the 1890 Lunacy Act'. Although the 1890 Act with its definition of only 'certified' patients remained in force, two new categories of 'voluntary' and 'temporary' patients were now added, and the categorisation process was dissociated from the Poor Law. No longer would all patients have to be 'certified' in order to be treated for mental illness. The new Act, based on the findings of the 1926 Royal Commission (the Macmillan Report), attempted to reconcile 'the conflict between the patient's need for treatment and the necessity of safeguarding his civil liberties'. Watkin writes that:

> At the time the Macmillan Commission were appointed there was a good deal of public uneasiness relating to the administration of the lunacy laws and allegations were being made both that large numbers of sane people were being detained as insane, and that cruelty was widespread in the public mental hospitals. ... The commissioners declared themselves well satisfied with the general standard of care in the twenty-five hospitals they visited and gave their opinion that 'the wholesale allegations of neglect and ill-treatment which are sometimes made in regard to the present system' were unjustified.

In addition to the important introduction of voluntary and temporary patients, the 1930 Act consigned the terms 'asylum' and 'lunatic' to history, and encouraged the provision of psychiatric out-patient clinics. The Act would ensure, a Government spokesman claimed in Parliament, that a doctor was 'not the sinister figure which in former times he was represented to be, anxious to confine a man in a dungeon for life'. But Watkin notes that there were limitations and drawbacks in putting the Act into practice:

> In most hospitals it was another three decades before a jangling bunch of keys ceased to be the symbol of office of the mental nurse. A less happy consequence of the Act was the emergence of two standards of accommodation, staffing and treament, with those wards set aside for voluntary patients becoming the showpieces

where the psychiatrists spent most of their time, and where the younger and more intelligent mental nurses were put to work.

In Wiltshire, out-patient clinics, as encouraged by the Act, had already been introduced. Wiltshire's Visiting Committee had supported a Board of Control recommendation, in line with the Macmillan Report, for 'mental clinics at general hospitals'. 'Such a system', they felt, 'has a great future before it, and promises in time a considerable reduction in the number of patients in institutions and a considerable relief to the rates'. Not only might 'incipient cases' avoid ever coming to the Mental Hospital, but also, 'the mental health inmate may benefit from the medical staff's widened experience and observation'. Furthermore, linking mental health work with general medicine would help 'lessen the stigma of lunacy'. In due course Cole was appointed Honorary Neurologist to Victoria Hospital, Swindon, and started weekly clinics there in January 1927. Leech began similar clinics at the Trowbridge Cottage Hospital soon after. By 1930, when seventy-five patients made 224 attendances, the clinics were assessed as 'useful as well as interesting ... [providing] a good deal of help to patients and their doctors'.

The Visiting Committee's 1931 report to Wiltshire County Council leaves no doubt that they felt that the new Act would prove a milestone in the life of the Hospital:

> The Committee hope that the possibilities of earlier treatment of mental disease given by this Act are becoming more known and appreciated both by the public and the medical practitioners. The Clinics held weekly at Swindon and Trowbridge have proved their value, and the Committee have engaged two ladies as Social Workers to keep in touch with all those who receive assistance from the medical staff, and with their families. This is at present the main source of expense incurred under the Act, and it is likely to prove one of the most valuable of the extended powers. The committee would like to appeal to all the medical practitioners in the county to get to understand, and then use as far as possible, the better facilities for earlier expert treatment which the Act offers, and which the Committee are anxious to put at their disposal. The importance of the early treatment of mental disease cannot be over-estimated, and indirectly the pressure upon the accommodation at the Hospital may be thereby relieved, by obviating the necessity of patients being sent there at all.

After a few years the Swindon and Trowbridge out-patient clinics were considered still to be making progress, though under-used because local GPs failed to understand their benefits. With other provisions of the 1930 Act, they had helped to open up the treatment of mental health beyond the walls of the

Mental Hospital. The two social workers, and sometimes the Hospital's own Medical Officers, were beginning to visit the homes of actual and prospective patients. The 'on trial' system, which had existed as part of the pre-release procedure for many decades, and which had in recent years been increasingly backed up by monetary grants, was now further extended to include the boarding out of patients 'in selected homes'. By April 1934 twenty females were boarded out 'with complete success', and a further ten females and ten males were to follow. The Committee reported, 'the experiment has attracted considerable attention in other quarters, and it is understood that several other committees are taking similar steps'.

The Visiting Committee was not entirely happy with the new arrangements. 'By virtue of the Mental Health Act', they grumbled in their Minutes, 'the Committee were now practically bound to accept certain patients direct from their homes'. The old cosy arrangement whereby they came only from the workhouse Unions was gone. With regard to temporary patients, the Committee considered that the new provision was not working, and had become 'a dead letter' by 1934, because its stipulations were 'inapplicable to all but cases of profound mental confusion'.

Admissions to the Hospital nevertheless included increasing proportions of voluntary patients (almost one-third in 1937 and 1938), a result credited by the Commissioners largely to the success of the out-patient clinics and the social workers. Throughout the 1930s the Commissioners were urging the development of Occupational Therapy schemes, which they had seen 'applied to recently admitted as well as to noisy, degraded and indolent patients with beneficial results'. 'Occupational training [for] some of the low-grade female patients' had been conducted by the Housekeeper since 1928, with what Cole considered 'very gratifying results'. By 1932 this work had expanded to involve over thirty female patients making 'all the female patients' dresses ... nurses' uniforms, aprons, sheets, and the men's shirts', plus 'basketry, rug-making, and making seats for stools and chairs'. But the Commissioners thought that 'the fringe of what is known as Occupational Therapy had hardly been touched'; the scheme needed 'considerable expansion and the facilities supporting it 'putting into much better order'. It could be used more 'towards recovery or towards the economic usefulness of patients who do not recover'.

Sydney Cole's twenty-one year reign as Medical Superintendent ended in 1934, when he retired following a period of serious illness. His deputy, Dr John Leech (otherwise Jack, or even, off the official record, 'Paddy'), was appointed as his successor. Dr Millar Speer, 'a young Ulsterman' who had been at the Hospital for ten years, was promoted to be Leech's deputy.

From Cole's autobiography, as from the reports of his period, we get the impression of an austere man, with an acerbic wit which he could turn against himself, highly diligent if conservative in his work with the mentally ill (though he was in the forefront of the establishment nationally of out-patient mental health clinics) and deeply immersed in the life of the town. He had papers published in prestigous medical journals and became president of the Wiltshire branch of the British Medical Association, which often held meetings in the Hospital's recreation hall. A keen amateur singer, conductor, composer and actor, he performed frequently as a baritone soloist in Devizes and at the Hospital, quoting some of the reviews (not only the favourable ones) in his journal. He was a prominent member of the Devizes Musical Association, and records with apparent distaste the fact that during the 1920s it 'had taken to Gibert and Sullivan'. His reaction to the change was to launch the breakaway Devizes Philharmonic Society to meet the need, as he saw it, for 'choral music of a higher kind'. Even so, he had thrown himself into the title role in *The Mikado* in 1923 to such effect that he was seen (as noted by Peggy Hancock, in David Buxton's *Devizes Voices*) as 'a real Mikado: even without make-up he looked the part'.

He would send his musical compositions to national figures such as Walford Davies for comment. He loved to hob-nob with such figures, and when Mr (later Sir) Adrian Boult came to adjudicate at the Devizes Music Festival, brought him to Campfield, his residence at the Hospital, for tea. But he was caught out in 1932 when, unknown to him, the composer Arnold Bax played cricket at the Hospital in a touring team run by his brother, the writer Clifford Bax. Cole was not interested in sport, and 'not knowing what interesting men they were, hadn't put in an appearance': he made sure he did so on their two subsequent visits.

*By permission of John Leech*

**Sydney Cole, with hat; Arnold Bax, with tie; Clifford Bax, with beard.**

Clifford Bax drew on his cricketing visits to the Hospital in a piece entitled *The Trousseau*, published in *Lovat Dickson's Magazine* in 1933.

\*     \*     \*     \*     \*

*We had won the toss and our first two batsmen were walking to the wickets, when the rest of us, lying back in deck-chairs within the pavilion enclosure, were surprised to hear a muffled trampling of many feet,- not the crisp crunch of a regiment marching but a sound more slovenly. We looked round and saw, with some curiosity, that the male inmates were filing from the County Mental Hospital to the cricket ground. We assumed, of course, that the two or three hundreds who gradually settled themselves on the wooden benches that encircled the playing-field were not dangerous, but the dreary vacuity of their faces and the inconsequence of their mutterings and movements made us uneasy and lowered our spirits.*

*Not one of those forlorn and shabby figures paid any attention to the game. Many of them did not even look at it. One, it is true, called out every few minutes: 'Boundary, boundary', although at the time our batsmen were quite unable to hit boundaries from the bowling of the two male nurses; and we noticed that none of the spectators conversed with one another. Each was marooned within his own disordered brain. A tall fellow, for instance, strode restlessly up and down a certain strip of grass, delivering an incoherent lecture, while, screwing up one of his eyes, he showed with pride how it was possible to hold a match in the creases of flesh which he thus made. There were, however, two patients who attracted our particular attention. The first was a portly double-chinned man, better dressed than the others, who never spoke a word, but remained, throughout the game, staring listlessly at the grass between his boots. The senior doctor, as it happened, was sitting among us, and from him we learned that this poor fellow had been a German doctor who, long before even the great war, had owned a good practice in the neighbourhood. His wife had gone off with another man, and within a few weeks he himself had entered the Mental Hospital. He had now been there, said our host, for twenty years, but in all that time had hardly spoken a word. Some visitors had once hoped to revive his earlier self by talking to him in German, but the patient's mind was in a fog so dense that nothing could pierce it. The other man who aroused our curiosity was of an opposite kind. He wore sand-shoes, trousers, a white shirt and a coloured handkerchief which he had wound about his head. To and fro he walked, at a smart pace, in front of those unresponsive benches, playing a mouth-organ, and at the same time juggling dexterously either with Indian clubs or a number of coloured balls. And all the while he kept up a running commentary as though he were addressing a breathless audience. We began to wonder how long he could endure the physical effort of this performance, seeing that for three-quarters of an hour he never stopped, but at last, quite suddenly, he drew himself up to attention, bowed and called out to the serried gargoyles who were sitting in front of him and paying him no heed, 'Ladies and gentlemen, that is the end. The evening performance will begin at nine o'clock sharp. Good-night, good-night!' With that, he packed up his toys in a knapsack which he placed on the ground, and lying with his head on it, pretended to go fast asleep: but within a few minutes up he jumped and began once more to throw and catch his clubs, never missing one of them, as he walked rapidly up and down.*

*'He does that all day', said the doctor,'and he is about the fittest man, physically, that I've ever seen. Not an ounce of fat on him. He was, of course, a professional - worked in the music-halls - but he has been here longer than I have, and I've been here ten years.'*

\*     \*     \*     \*     \*

Because of Cole's musical involvement, but even more so because of the interest, talent and vivacity of his wife Dot, twenty years his junior, the programme of entertainments at the hospital during their time was a very full one. Plays, pantomimes and concerts abounded, usually by staff for patients, and often repeated outside the Hospital for various charities. Mrs Cole led a pierrot troupe in 1929, and seems to have excelled even herself in February 1930, when she produced, directed and conducted a Staff Concert Party for the patients, which included 'strings, wind, percussion, pianoforte, and jazz instruments ... three sketches and a circus ... burlesques on the tight-rope walker and the bare-back rider, and the performing elephants and seals'. Cole, despite his preference, as we have seen, for 'music of a higher kind', seems to have approved.

John Leech (junior) highlights the different character of the three Superintendents he knew best:

> Bowes, Cole, Leech - the three doctors had little in common: Bowes the benevolent autocrat, fond of shooting game, totally absorbed in asylum administration. Cole, the intellectual, lover of books, music, chess, learned in the psychology of the insane. Leech, clever with his hands, boisterous, lover of sailing-ships, motor cars, horses, cats and practical jokes.

By the mid-1930s, with Dr Jack Leech established as Medical Superintendent, a range of new facilities for patients was being provided. The 'talking cinema apparatus' was already very popular. A canteen started two years before had doubled in size by 1935 and had been extended to include a tea house and a lending library with reading room; it provided 'a place for patients to be with visiting friends and relatives'. Football and cricket teams exclusively for patients were established, while the women had facilities for badminton and hockey, and also a pipe band. The number of patients granted parole outside the Hospital grounds was gradually being increased, fifty qualifying for this freedom by 1937.

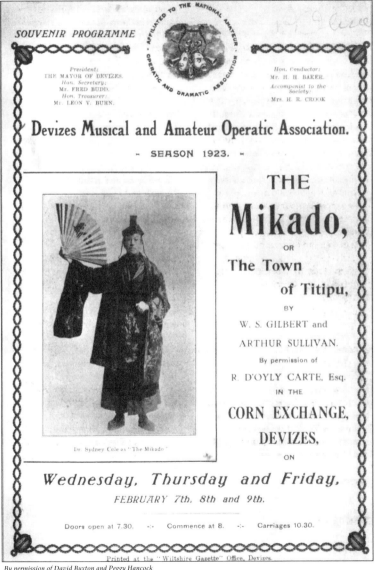

By permission of David Buxton and Peggy Hancock

**Dr Sydney Cole as The Mikado**

# THE
# PALACE
## DEVIZES

# WEDNESDAY, FEB. 17th, 1932
## at 4 and 8 p.m.

Tickets obtainable only from the Palace. 'Phone 171.
Book Your Seats Early!

## AMATEUR PERFORMANCE OF
## GRAND PANTOMIME

# THE
# SLEEPING
# BEAUTY

### By Members of the Staff of the Wilts County Mental Hospital.

In aid of the Funds of the Mental After Care Association for the assistance of poor persons convalescent or recovered from institutions for the insane.

STAFF

| | | |
|---|---|---|
| Prince Rudolf | | E. LAKE |
| The Princess | | N. WISE |
| The King | | A. E. TURNER |
| The Queen | | M. WHALE |
| Master of Hounds | | A. HAINES |
| Goldilocks | | A. E. BEAVIS |
| Hyacinth | | R. W. JOHNSON |
| The King's Physician | | A. E. BLAGDON |
| The Fairy Queen | | G. W. PEPLER |
| The Witch | | L. SHORT |
| Master of Ceremonies | | L. STAGG |
| Nurse | | D. WILD |
| Sentry | | G. SHORT |
| Bluebell (Hounds of ) | | L. STAGG |
| Harkaway (the Pack ) | | D. WILD |

Chorus:—Misses M. Baker, P. Huntley, V. Bennet, M. Whitbread, K. Doran, K. Butler, W. Dunn, G. Rudd, C. Evans.

SCENES

| | |
|---|---|
| PROLOGUE | THE FOREST |
| ACT I. | THE KING'S CASTLE |
| ACT II. | OUTSIDE THE MAGIC WOOD |
| ACT III. (1) | THE CASTLE THE AWAKENING |
| (2) | |
| (3) | THE CASTLE |

*By permission of WRO*

# 13 - A Stuffed Emu and an Antique Piano

Apicture of Hospital life at this time is given by Ronnie Newman, who started work there as an attendant in 1934. His grandmother had become 'lady's maid' to Mrs Thurnam, wife of the first Superintendent, in 1852. His maternal grandfather had been Head Tailor at the Asylum, and his father became Deputy Head Attendant, a post equivalent to the one later attained by Ronnie himself. The period between Ronnie's father's death in 1923 and his own arrival was the only break in the Newman family's service there through to its closure. He recorded his recollections, some in the form of notes for an intended autobiography and others in a duplicated pamphlet entitled *Ronnie's Reminiscences*, which circulated in the years leading up to his retirement in 1980. He expressed justifiable confidence that his writing would be 'of interest to a generation that will no doubt read what I have to say'. Presumably drawing on family recollections as well as Asylum records and artefacts, he noted that when he had started at the hospital, things had changed little since its opening:

> The food had possibly improved and its presentation; perhaps more parole - patients in the grounds, the clothing quite unchanged. The rewards for work - tobacco for men, sweets for women were still the same as the 1850s. The furnishings in the wards were unchanged from that time, also the staff disciplines were as always. Uniform for instance was unchanged since the introduction in the mid-19th Century, the only change here was the old Crimea type hat was replaced in the 1920s by a 1914 soldier type of headgear. ... The uniform was of heavy and dark serge, the brass buttons duly stamped Wilts County Asylum, [and] a strong leather belt attached to which was a brass chain with keys and whistles attached.
>
> I reported for duty on April 9th 1934. ... At the lodge I was duly escorted to the Head Attendant's office and then handed over to Bertie Adams the Charge Attendant of Male 1 [later Beech Ward]. This ward had changed but little since the 1850s being a ward that accommodated the well behaved and tidy patients, the furnishings were much varied - there was an old Grandfather Clock with solid brass face, a stuffed emu and an antique piano. As in all wards the tables were solid pine with iron footrests, it would take four strong

men to lift them and they were covered after meals with green baize cloths. There were a couple of basketwork armchairs, all the other seating was solid pine forms and open coal fires which we 'Last Hands', as we were called, had to light each morning.

As an aside the fire precautions were almost nil, we used to light the fires with wax cloths that were used on the floor - this wax was a combination of beeswax and turpentine made up in the Painter's Yard. It had a pleasing smell and every ward floor was soaked in this highly inflammable mixture.

The walls were covered in large framed pictures such as Landseer and other Victorian artists and cases of stuffed birds, foxes, rabbits etc. This was the best ward in the Main Building but the furnishings in other wards were reduced to the bare minimum of requirements the reason of course was the constant threat of violence - chairs, pictures, plants (the aspidistra was the favourite) would all be used as weapons so the Refractory and Semi-Refractory Wards had the heavy tables and forms and a few horsehair lined heavy sofas.

The old photographs show the Attendants wearing a type of bow tie to prevent, of course, manual strangulation. ... The Strong Suits for men and dresses for women were of strong sail canvas

*Photographed at Glenside Hospital Museum by P Steele*

**Strong Clothing**

locked on by cylinder locks as were the boots. The side rooms were about 8' x 5' with high shutters, windows that had sloping sills, a mattress on the floor with a canvas blanket, although if the patient was destructive the mattress was removed. A type of fibre-glass chamber pot was all that the room contained and often this was removed. There were cases of patients who spent 20 years in such rooms.

Force feeding was legal and frequently practised. I remember seeing an old Pot and Caustic stick being used on the penis to prevent masturbation. This barbaric practice had been used right into the 20th Century. Also still in situ in the Male Refractory Wards was a corner Water Cupboard with just enough room for the man to stand up in, the door was locked and cold water was turned on the unfortunate patient, the water running to waste through a drain at the man's feet. ...

The first years of my service were spent on the Airing Courts where we walked the walls two hours in the morning and one and a half hours in the afternoon. At the end of that summer I was a bronzed and fit young man. Windows were often smashed and some bad cuts resulted, boots were also used as weapons and ... had to be locked up. All clothes of course were institutional cords for trousers with heavy tweed jackets, the smell in the always crowded dormitories in the summer was awful. Shaving was one of the miserable jobs, the blades issued were poor quality and often inadequate in number, many patients used pumice stone and rubbed their beards down rather than undergo the misery of a blunt blade. We used to do our best by rubbing the blades around the inside of a tumbler glass to sharpen them.

There is no need for me to elaborate on treatment as we know in this modern age there were none and when a patient became disturbed we called it 'up the pole'. A three-quarter pint mug was filled with what we called White Draught which was of course Mist. Alb., a vicious purge.

The eating utensils were all enamel and tea was consumed from enamel pudding basins, knives were only used on Sundays (blunt as a piece of cloth) and forks had tinns only a quarter-inch in length, spoons were the general order for all meals. We had to cut all the bread by hand, half-inch slices from huge loaves we had to collect from the hospital bakery. The food was plain and nourishing and it would be true to say that many poor families of the 1930s would have considered themselves well fed on the patients' diet.

Ronnie Newman's family, like those of many employees at the Hospital, had lived in Potterne. They came and went via a path through the cemetery, opening the gate with a pass key. He recalls hearing as a child the Hospital's steam whistle, which was 'still blowing away up to 1929. It was then used once a day only - at 12.45 pm - for patients' and staff dinner. Villagers would adjust their clocks to its sound'. In the Hospital itself there was 'the clock over the Lodge entrance which overlooks the courtyard'; from there a bell 'with its red and white "Sally" ... was used from 6.30 am to 10.30 pm throughout the year, and it governed the life of the hospital'.

Newman writes that they had to get up at 5.30am to light fires and then get the patients' breakfast; normal 'bed-up' time for patients was 6.30pm, but 'patients working on the land were allowed to sit up until 8.30pm in the Workers' Ward'. This sets in context a comment made in the Commissioners' report on their 1938 visit, a three-day affair, commending the 'considerate care' of the staff and management, and giving as an example, 'A privilege ... to sit up until about 9pm, a cup of tea or coffee and something to eat being given to about sixty female and one hundred male patients'. It is clear that the great majority of patients - those who were neither 'workers' nor 'privileged' - went at least from 6pm to 6am with no provision at all for their sustenance. It was not until 1947 that the need for a supper meal was seriously addressed.

There was little relief for the patients from the Hospital routine; Newman could 'only remember one "outside" activity' in his early days:

> That was the 'Good Friday Walk' when about 100 patients were taken, via the Cemetery, over 'One Tree Hill', and returned via Green Lane. The patients may have enjoyed this brief glimpse of the outside world, but for the staff ... it was an hour of tension in case we lost anyone. The inside activities were mainly cricket and football, staff concert parties, the weekly patients' dance (winter only) and the weekly cinema.

Contemporary reports by the Commissioners paint a slightly less bleak picture, however. Fifteen male patients had parole outside the grounds in 1936, and in addition to the activities mentioned by Newman, there was a women's pipe band, a folk dancing class, several small garden plots cultivated by patients, and a staff band. Ronnie Newman must have been exercising undue modesty, since he was a trombonist in the latter.

Newman was present when the foundation stone was laid in 1937 for the new separate, purpose-built chapel, after decades of cajoling from the Commissioners. It was, and remains, a handsome building, though it surprisingly held only 200 people, which was fewer than its much-criticised predecessor. The old chapel in the main building had been above the kitchen:

> On Sunday afternoons in the summer we used to roast from the heat arising from below and the heat of the leaden roofs - there was little need for the Chaplain to preach on Hell fire; we felt we were

at the gates! A rather naughty trick on such afternoons was for an Attendant to kick the pews and let out a yell, then an unsuspecting patient was suddenly carried from Chapel, apparently in a fit. We would pick patients who would 'help' in the intrigue knowing they would be rewarded with a smoke.

Set in the chapel porch was an ancient stone, which Dr Thurnam had 'brought down from Gore's Cross, above West Lavington' around the 1870s, and which had stood for decades outside the old Asylum cemetery chapel. (It was thought to be Saxon, but more recent opinion places it as mediaeval, and probably originating from Old Sarum.) The Visiting Committee noted that, 'a patient who had for several years taken no interest in anything, and had come to be regarded as probably incurable, devoted himself to the care of the interior, and in a few months' time was discharged as recovered'.

By permission of WRO

*Hospital Chapel - Dedicated 1937*

*Main entrance, from Pans Lane*

# 14 - Convulsion Therapy and Brain Surgery

Sanitation continued to be a problem throughout the 1930s, with TB and dysentery always present to some degree. Since the vast Victorian complex would soon need to undergo major reorganisation and building work, it was considered uneconomical to attack the problem piecemeal. A major scheme was approved and funded in 1935 and in addition to the new chapel, was to include a major reorganisation of the main block, providing for:

- Ward space for defined classes of patients.
- Clinical rooms for each ward.
- Cloak rooms and patients' clothing storerooms.
- An operating theatre, x-ray room and dispensary.
- Additional patient accommodation.
- A mess room for staff.

*By permission of John Leech*

*Dr J. F. W. Leech*

Despite delays caused by new sanitary regulations, a start was made within a couple of years, but in 1939 war intervened. History repeated itself, and the outbreak of war, as it had in 1914, caused a major building project for the improvement of the Hospital to be suspended indefinitely.

Another early effect of war conditions, again as in 1914, was an influx of evacuated patients. From Park Prewett in Hampshire 220 came, then in 1941 sixty-seven more from Brookwood, Surrey and Knowle, Hampshire. The total number of patients exceeded 1400, and because of the risk of bombing, all of those in the main building slept on the ground floor. This was, of course, a sensible precaution, though in the event only one bomb fell anywhere near the Hospital throughout the war, in a field half a mile away. John Leech (junior) writes of his father ordering £100 worth of blackout material for curtains, experimenting by painting the hospital blinds black, and supervising a firewatcher's post on the highest roof. He also tells of an ingenious method of escape from the upper floors in the event of fire, by a rope and harness device; it was tested by himself as a twenty-year-old, managing to put both feet through matron's window on the way down, and the bulky Dr Millar Speer who, though trussed up like 'a very large parcel' and doing no good to his best gloves, enjoyed the experience so much that he wanted to try it again.

In the midst of the chaotic wartime conditions, however, one of the most significant steps was taken in the treatment of patients at the Hospital. The first purchase of equipment for electro-convulsive therapy (ECT) was made in 1942. Between the wars a range of new treatments had been developed, and mental hospitals had introduced them at their own pace and with varying degrees of success. Wiltshire was one of the slower to make these innovations, concentrating rather on its successful programme of out-patient clinics and social work. New continuous bath facilities were being installed in 1939, for example, when other hospitals were abandoning the practice. Some of the treatments which became generally available are described by Eric Pryor.

> - **Therapeutic Malaria.** Used for General Paralysis of the Insane (GPI), which accounted for about ten per cent of admissions and was a result of syphilis. The patient was inoculated 'either by a bite from a malaria-carrying mosquito or by injecting him with infected blood. ... The resultant rigors - providing treatment was given in the early stages - arrested the disease. The malaria was terminated by the administration of quinine'.

> - **Convulsion Therapy**. 'Used mainly for certain types of depressive illness. A drug was injected ... [usually Cardiazol] ... to induce an epileptiform seizure. This treatment was the forerunner of the more sophisticated Electro-Convulsive Therapy'.

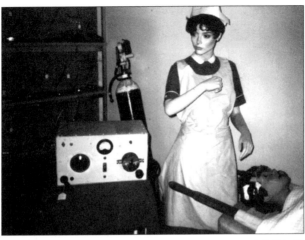

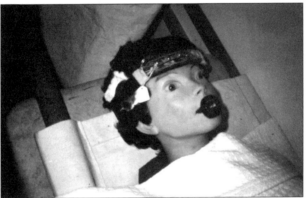

*Photographed at Glenside Hospital Museum by P Steele*
**Early ECT Equipment c.1940**

Malarial therapy had been started at Claybury in 1923. Wiltshire's Commissioners reported in 1930 that it was not in use here, but it had been introduced by 1938. Ronnie Newman recalls that the mosquito bite was used and that he 'would spend the night wrapping the patient in wet sheets for reduction of temperature'. Malarial treament was continued until at least the late 1940s, but a study quoted in *The Social Organization of Mental Illness*, by Lindsay Prior, found it to be only twenty-five per cent effective.

In 1938 the Commissioners noted that 'treatment by cardiazol has been commenced among male patients and has produced one or two excellent results'. But the following year two patients sustained fractures during convulsive treatment. Newman's account of the treatment is a negative one:

I was selected for the team. The treatment consisted of a darkened room (why I don't know); the patient was strapped to a stretcher (on legs); a tourniquet was placed on the arm and the Cardiazol injected by the doctor. The tourniquet was removed and the patient had a violent epileptic fit. The experiment was discarded after a short time.

ECT was given to seventy-six patients in the first year. Leech wrote that 'the general results have been most satisfactory, and in some cases of great benefit'. In 1944, ECT was 'now being given to selected female patients. The best results are being obtained in cases of depression associated with the menopause. On the male side, the results of this form of treatment have been less encouraging'. But 'good results' were again claimed in 1946.

In that year Leech introduced to the Hospital a revolutionary brain surgery treatment for which encouraging results were being claimed elsewhere. Known as pre-frontal leucotomy, it was performed 'at the hands of the local consulting surgeon'. It was considered suitable for patients 'severely incapacitated by a long standing mental illness which other treatments had failed to alleviate'. Eric Pryor observes:

> Their illness was often much less distressing to them, and to those around them, after the operation. But the criticism was that many patients were post-operatively emotionally blunted, about a third of them seriously, and the results were irreversible'.

Despite wartime strictures and overcrowding (the number of patients reaching an all-time peak of 1510 in August 1943), reports show a 'business as usual' approach. The minutiae of Hospital life were still matters for concern. The Commissioners were concerned that a patient had been wearing the same pair of socks for several weeks. Leech had to adjudicate over an attendant who had tried to appropriate a patient's £102 pools win. The Matron 'refused to hand over her electric fire as requested' and had to be persuaded by the Chairman. An Assistant Medical Officer, serving in India, sent 'a very violent Cable' complaining that his wife had been persuaded to share her accommodation at the Hospital with another AMO and his wife. Staff was short, and parole outside the grounds was a problem due to 'frequent interrogation by the military for purposes of indentification'. But no serious health problems arose like those experienced in World War I; on the contrary, the long battle against TB and dysentery seems to have been almost won.

The Commissioners commented in 1944 on the 'friendly atmosphere' between staff and patients; 'It is not often that we have the pleasure of visiting a mental hospital ... where there are so few complaints from patients and where a general feeling of contentment is so evident'.

# 15 - Bach and Mozart

When the war ended, things took some years to return to normal. Of nearly 300 evacuees, 117 were still present in 1947, when the number of patients had reduced only to 1338. The much-needed building and redecoration programme could not yet be resurrected since the plans may have had to be 'entirely or very largely recast' because of the revolutionary provisions of the 1946 National Health Act. Even so, estimates were sent to the Ministry of Health for a resumption of the scheme, with further provision for nursing accommodation and for repair work which was long overdue.

This was the discouraging position when Dr Jack Leech retired in 1947 after forty-one years on the staff, the final thirteen as Medical Superintendent. He was 'much beloved', the Commissioners commented, and his 'geniality and kindliness helped to solve many difficulties'. As he himself had done, and Cole before him, his Deputy, Dr Millar Speer, now stepped up to the top job. The

*By permission of WRO*

*Dr J. M. C. Speer*

Commissioners were 'glad to find him so fully aware of [the Hospital's] many needs', but this was hardly surprising, since he had already been there for twenty-three years.

The introduction of the National Health Service does not seem to have had a profound immediate effect. The most obvious was the change of name on 16 June 1948 to Roundway Hospital. (Some committee members pointed out that the name was misleading, since Roundway village was on the other side of Devizes. They would have preferred Wick Green Hospital, but did not get their way.) County mental hospitals were no longer to be the responsibilty of local government but of regional boards under the Ministry of Health. The South West Regional Hospital Board's new Hospital Management Committee (HMC) for Roundway consisted almost entirely of members of the County Council's disbanding Visiting Committee. The one newcomer was the Chairman, Dr A C Mowle, a Devizes consulting surgeon who undertook routine minor surgery for Roundway, while stalwart supporters of the Hospital such as Miss M F Awdry the Vice-Chairman, Lady Katharine McNeile and Mr George Ward continued their work. Though this Committee acknowledged Roundway to be handicapped by 'conditions which should not exist in a hospital', and though parts of the long-delayed project for modernisation and reorganisation were given Regional approval, little happened in practice; improvements were 'in abeyance' in 1950, and though some were 'pressing ahead' by 1953, advancement was still only 'piecemeal' in 1954.

*Hospital Management Committee, 1948. Standing: Mr G Ward, Dr J M C Speer, Mr J F Beaven, Mr R S Gilbey, Mr E J Couzens, Mr F Swanton. Sitting: Mrs Tonge, Miss M F Awdry (Vice-Chairman), Dr A C Mowle (Chairman), Mr W J Rendell, Lady Katharine McNeile.*

The Board of Control Commissioners, making their first visit of inspection under the NHS in 1949, found shabbily clothed patients, overcrowded conditions and a 'grave shortage of nurses' on the female wards. But they thought the kitchen 'a modern and well-equipped unit', and listed a wide range of activities and entertainments for patients, including weekly dances, frequent concerts, billiard tournaments, cricket, football, bowls, and tennis on a new court.

Centralised organisation was beginning to take a hand in the entertainment programme. The Council for Music in Hospitals 'sent musicians in full evening dress to play Bach and Mozart to the patients'. Perhaps unsurprisingly, the *Roundway Review* found a 1953 concert 'a little too technical and the songs in German a little too tedious', but a piano recital two months later earned glowing praise, and the leading English tenor of the day, Heddle Nash, sang at Roundway in 1955. Visits by sporting celebrities were also organised, notably a billiards and snooker demonstration in 1956 by Horace Lindrum.

The Hospital farm was still active, providing produce for its residents and work for some of the patients. In 1950 there were 53 cows, supplying the Hospital with 33,000 gallons of milk, 288 pigs fattened and sold, and good crops of fruit and vegetables, hay, corn and roots. But the farm was being plagued by an arsonist, with four fires in a few months in the hay barn in 1948-9. A fifth followed in 1950, but whether the arsonist was ever caught is not minuted. Partly in response to these fires, the HMC boosted the Hospital's fire service to a twenty-strong Fire Brigade. Membership was compulsory for all resident male staff under forty, and non-resident staff could volunteer; all were paid an extra £5 a year.

A 'great increase' in social work was reported in 1948, a third worker being appointed. The three devoted 'much of their time to the work of the Clinics, obtaining case histories, assisting and advising patients and relatives, [and] the follow-up of patients leaving Hospital ...'. The new appointee was Miss Gweneth Helliar, who recalls that she had taken courses in psychology and her interest was known to Dr and Mrs Speer, who knew her mother, so despite having no paper qualifications, she got the job. Very little was known of the families of in-patients, even by the patients themselves, particularly if they had been in Hospital a long time, so case histories had to be built up from scratch. Some families hardly ever visited - if the family might have been partially to blame for the patient's condition it was not encouraged - but others visited very diligently, 'especially the Gypsies'. She acted as a 'prop' for out-patients between their visits to the psychiatrist, including some women who had come seeking a termination of pregnancy on psychiatric grounds and had been refused. On her first Christmas Day at Roundway, the tour of the wards which all officers were expected to make took her into the refractory wards for the first time. She was surprised to find the women there in 'strong dresses' of canvas with buckles and straps. All the wards were locked at that time, though some began to be left unlocked soon after.

In 1951 the death of Dr Jack Leech, only four years after his retirement, was reported. Ronnie Newman recalls that, as a Junior Charge Attendant, he was among the 'Attendants in full uniform [who] pushed the old hand bier from the Cottage Hospital Mortuary to the Cemetery Chapel'. A bronze memorial plaque in the Hospital Chapel was unveiled on Palm Sunday 1953. Only two years later a plaque was offered to the Chapel by the recently widowed Dot Cole in memory her husband, Leech's predecessor.

The resignation from the HMC of Miss M F Awdry in 1954 was a significant stage in the gradual movement away from nurturing of the Hospital by a devoted local Wiltshire team to a more remote and impersonal form of bureaucratic control. Miss Awdry had served on the Visiting Committee and HMC for twenty-nine years, and was Chairman from 1950 to 1953. Dr Speer noted in his Centenary Report that her grandfather, Sir John Wither Awdry, had been Chairman of the Committee which considered the original project to establish the Asylum in 1846 and had served on the Committee until 1878. The eroding tradition of a family-style committee and a fatherly Medical Superintendent who ran the Hospital as a benevolent autocracy was within the next few years to be broken completely. Gweneth Helliar recalls that Speer 'had his finger absolutely on the spot. He knew literally every patient by name. He was very progressive; all the major changes were started by him.' But he was the last Medical Superintendent. When he retired in 1957 after thirty-two years at the Hospital, his successor, Dr J B Gordon-Russell, was designated Physician Superintendent. This may have seemed merely a subtle change of terminology, but only seven years later, when Gordon-Russell left, no head person at all was appointed. His functions were to be filled by a process of 'consultation and co-operation ... co-ordination and planning' which took half a page of the minute book to define. The Chairman of the Medical Advisory Committee, 'his medical colleagues', 'heads of departments', and an extra, newly-appointed Consultant Psychiatrist would all be involved. It was to be government by committee, and by Regional Board.

# 16 - A Fried Egg for Christmas

The *Roundway Review* was a booklet published monthly by the HMC, with the chaplain's office responsible editorially. It started in 1952 in typescript and crudely duplicated, but within a year appeared in an attractive printed format with an aerial photograph of the Hospital on the cover. As well as circulating within the Hospital it was available outside, initially at a cost of threepence a copy, but from 1955 free. Both staff and patients contributed articles of a high quality, the most frequent being Rev J O Dobson, a recovered former patient who had become the nonconformist Chaplain, and Eric Walrond, a patient who served as Assistant Editor. Some articles were fictional but others aired current affairs and mental health matters from a wider viewpoint than the purely parochial. Life at Roundway was a main theme of material from many contributors. Patients' outings to such destinations as Winchester, Stourhead and Stratford on Avon are described, plus outings by the choir, of which most of the members were patients. The *Review* could be an outlet for occasional bouts of bickering between sections of the staff, such as arguments about fund-raising for extra amenities. Reports of concerts and sporting events appear, and many random glimpses of Hospital life:

- The popularity of canaries in the wards is increasing and six more pairs have been introduced.
- The Hospital's Carnival and Sports Day are held as a combined event for the first time. (The Carnival in 1953 had been a big enough event to include the Dagenham Girl Pipers, the Wiltshire Regiment Band as well as the Hospital's own band, and displays by the Portsdown Archery Club, Broadleas School Players and Devizes Boy Scouts.)
- 200 patients go to a pantomime matinee in Devizes.
- One of many poems, *Song of Tribute,* by *Young Marlburian*, includes these verses:

> With patients for bathing and shaving and shock,
> Plus dozens of doorways to shut up and lock,
> The grass must be cut, the coal must be fetched.
> The sick patients' temperatures taken and sketched.

Their shoes must be polished, their ties must be straight.
They dare not get dirty when cleaning the grate.
There are needles to sharpen before they inject
The patient who is frightened and standing erect.

- Open fireplaces are being replaced by oil central heating.
- In a 'new approach to colour therapy', wards are being redecorated in 'cream and pastel shades' to replace the 'institutional green'. [However, comparable claims had been made periodically for nearly a hundred years.]
- Roundway cricket team wins the West of England Inter-Mental Hospital Cup in 1956, as it had in 1948. A staunch batsman in the team is the groundsman, Harry Palmer. His son Kenneth is appointed to the staff of Somerset County Cricket Club, and works as a ward orderly during the close season. [After his playing career with Somerset, Ken Palmer became a distinguished test-match umpire.]
- The 'Annexe Lecture and Debating Society' hears talks by patients on subjects from their own experience, including swimming, rugby, making train buffer springs, and parachuting into Jugoslavia in the war (including, it is claimed, meeting Tito and capturing a German general).
- A local newspaper headline is quoted: 'Christmas at Roundway Lasts Six Weeks! - Happy Time at County Mental Hospital'.
- A League of Friends is formed for Roundway.

Staff of Roundway, and of the Pewsey Colony, which for some years had been caring for certain categories of chronic mentally ill, took part in a mental nursing exhibition in Trowbridge in 1956. Entitled 'The Challenge', it was aimed both at nursing recruitment and generally informing the public about the mental health services. The *Roundway Review* reported the event, but not the further fact, discussed by the HMC, that the health service trade union, COHSE, had threatened a boycott and demonstration, which was averted by their being allowed to distribute literature in the hall. Union power, wielded firstly by the Asylum Workers' Union and later by COHSE, had been a factor in the Hospital since 1920, and while some militancy from time to time is evident, in line with the social pattern of the day, it does seem, as claimed by Ronnie Newman as Branch Secretary of COHSE, to have achieved real improvements in staff conditions.

A *Review* Editorial in 1956 surely relates to the same patient who had inspired Clifford Bax's pen more than twenty years earlier:

*       *       *       *       *

*It is doubtful if there has ever been a more colourful personality at Roundway than Harry, particularly in his more flamboyant days, and his passing this month at the age of sixty-five has left a vacant place among the fast diminishing coterie of 'old-timers' that will never be filled. For Harry, Music Hall artiste, brought with him when he was first admitted as a patient in 1919 all the colour and liveliness of the theatre: an irrepressible urge to perform that was to bring him to the forefront of all Hospital activities and entertainments during the thirty-six years of his stay.*

*On the cricket field and football ground, at staff concerts and patients' performances Harry delved into his repertoire to produce his Harlequin dress for tumbling displays, or his juggling clubs that faithfully provided the piece de resistance on many occasions. The zither and the mouth organ, often combined were never far from reach and on many a warm summer evening the strains of a catchy tune or poignant melody could be heard from the distance where a solitary figure played quietly for his own pleasure.*

*But there was also a purpose and resourcefulness behind the artistry and over a number of years many charities benefitted from the collections that grew from the 'passing of the hat' not least of which were the Guide Dogs for the Blind Association and the Roundway Hospital Football Club on whose behalf, Harry was an ardent and practical 'supporter'.*

*In sporting activities Harry took part with gusto; on occasions such as the Patients' Sports he entered every avaliable event, and who will forget his invariable and elaborate 'tumble' with which he always ended his sack race.*

*Now the music has stopped and the zither stands among the other 'props' in one of the dressing rooms off the Recreation Hall stage, silent reminders of a very colourful and entertaining companion.*

*       *       *       *       *

A 1957 article by 'Dobbie', ie Rev J O Dobson, itemised some of the changes he had seen 'both in the wards and outside'. He had been at one time the only patient with a parole card, and so had 'quite a lot of errands to do'. The food was much better and varied:

> Every day of the week the menu used to stay the same, now we have a menu worked out with lots of surprises. There were great rejoicings when we first had a rasher of bacon for breakfast, and a fried egg on fried bread for Christmas, now we take it for granted. We now have a cooked supper, something different every evening.

If any of the patients wished to sit up in the Annexes 1 and 2, a nurse would take us down to Villa 2 at 7 o'clock and bring us back at 9 o'clock, no one could stay up in these wards being the admission wards. Now there is television in all three wards so naturally they can sit up. ...

All the patients who work get paid accordingly with tokens. When I first came it was a printed paper token to be spent at the Canteen...

Gradually each ward is having a nice new kitchen built from a room adjoining the dining room. The meals are handed out through the hatchway, this saves a lot of work in the wards.

In the previous issue Dobson had dealt with a weightier topic, of national as well as local significance. It was an action, reported in the national press, in which a patient who had incurred injuries while unconscious during ECT treatment was refused damages against Friern Mental Hospital, London. Dobson summarised the evidence given, and expressed some sympathy with expert opinion given to the jury, that 'Today a man suffering from some particular types of mental disorder had a real chance of recovery, ... that was due almost entirely to physical methods of treatment, of which ECT was the most important'. The judge had quoted Lord Denning, in an earlier case, to the effect that ECT, like many of the benefits of medical science, had conferred great benefits on mankind, and we could not take the benefits without the risks.

# 17 - Tranquillising Drugs

In the late 1940s another new treatment had been introduced. Selected schizophrenia sufferers were injected with doses of insulin to produce a coma. Early forms of the treatment might maintain the coma, with breaks for toilet and feeding, for fourteen days, but a modified and less invasive insulin therapy was introduced, requiring a much shorter period of unconsciousness, perhaps a few hours. Insulin treatment was supervised, under Speer's direction, by Bill Greenaway, who had taken extensive training and had become highly qualified in mental nursing, as well as gaining valuable experience in tropical medicine while on army war service in West Africa. It was found to improve the prospects of recovery and cut short the length of the attack. Both Greenaway and Bridget (Melody) Styche, who was then Matron, were and remain believers in its efficacy, feeling that it had a justified place in psychiatric treatment at the time. Greenaway does concede, however, that it could be

*By permission of Pinecraven Ltd*
### Dr J B Gordon-Russell

dangerous unless very close attention was paid to the patient throughout, and a range of possible problems anticipated. On the departure of the Hospital's Sister-Tutor, Bill Greenaway succeeded her in the job, thus becoming the first male Sister-Tutor at Roundway, and possibly in the whole country. It was not very long before the job-title was changed to the prosaic 'Tutor in Sole Charge'.

As regards other physical treatments, though the antiquated continuous bath equipment was eventually been removed in 1954, both ECT and pre-frontal leucotomy were well tried and in regular use for appropriate patients. Speer found ECT 'a most useful form of treatment for depressed patients, and, with careful selection of patients, safe and effective; for certain patients, 'curare [was] used to minimise as much as possible the muscular spasm'. ECT was used for out-patients, for whom clinics were by now being held at Salisbury and Devizes as well as Swindon and Trowbridge. Speer's 1953 Report noted that 'confident reliance' was still placed on ECT 'with relaxants', and on 'insulin shock therapy', while psychotherapy was practised extensively, but pre-frontal leucotomy, to which he had recently attributed 'much success', was not mentioned. Later references to leucotomy are wary, referring to 'carefully selected cases', a modified form of the operation, and the death of a patient in 1958 following the operation. As regards ECT, the strong foundation of Speer's 'confident reliance' was further built on by the progressive and innovative Gordon-Russell, who sought an extension in its use as one of his first acts as Physician Superintendent.

What was to prove the most significant development in treatment in the Hospital's history, however, is found in a mundane 1959 minute noting a large increase in expenditure on 'tranquillising drugs'. There was an 'important compensation', it was noted, in the 'reduced amount of clothing and furnish-

*By permission of Bill and Bridget Styche*

**Bill Greenaway in front of the Hospital**

By permission of Bill and Bridget Styche
*Devizes MP, Percival Pott with Dr Gordon-Russell, Mrs H. Wiltshire (Matron),*
*Bill Styche, Mr George Ward (HMC Chairman) and Mr A. E. Beavis (Chief Male Nurse) - 1957.*

ings which were damaged or destroyed', and furthermore, the expenditure 'was not likely to rise much further'. It is clear that the far greater compensation was not yet evident, that the number of mental patients whose illness could be controlled or perhaps even cured would rise dramatically, and that the number needing to stay in hospital would correspondingly fall. Eric Pryor explains that:

> This vast range of drugs, which appeared in the 1950s - the phenothiazine group, the so-called major tranquillisers, during 1955 and 1956, and the anti-depressant drugs in 1959 - dramatically altered the treatment of the major psychoses and gradually replaced almost all the physical treatments; not always because they were shown to be more effective but because they were equally efficacious and did not involve the same manpower and hazards and they were also believed to be reversible in their effects, or so it seemed in the 1950s. They certainly reduced the severity and duration of many conditions and created a setting where normalisation could flourish.

The first of these drugs in general use was largactil, which Gweneth Helliar recalls as the first to be used at Roundway. Kathleen Jones explains in *Asylums and After* that it enabled patients under stress to relax, though remaining fully conscious, and could thus relieve their more distressing symptoms while leaving them accessible to other forms of therapy. But she argues that the benefits of the new drugs, great as they may have been, were limited, and tempered with new problems:

> The new drugs were soon being widely prescribed. Within the mental hospitals, they created a totally different atmosphere. There was no longer any justification for 'refractory' wards, for wired-in airing courts, for strong-arm tactics on the part of staff. The more distressing sights of mental hospital wards - patients erupting into fits of violence, fighting off imaginary enemies, cowering in corners, or actively hallucinating, simply ceased to exist. Some patients were able to go home sooner; some did not need to enter hospital at all, since their symptoms could be controlled and their illness treated while they remained at home. The emphasis began to shift from talk of 'pre-care' and 'after-care' to talk of 'alternative care'.
>
> In the early days, the new drugs were prescribed very freely, and there was much optimism among psychiatrists. Only gradually was it realised that the phenothiazines alleviated, but did not cure. The symptoms were suppressed, but there were often marked side-effects, and the causes remained untouched. By 1961, Professor Morris Carstairs noted in *The Practitioner* that 'Few would claim that our current wonder drugs exercise anything more tha a palliative influence on psychiatric disorders. The big change has been rather one of public opinion'.

For many years the number of patients at Roundway had remained in the 1300s. The assumption by Old Manor, Salisbury, of responsibility for mental health patients in that part of the County had helped to keep numbers at Roundway in check. Some reduction was seen from 1956, partly due to the opening of Old Park House for some 'female patients, whose mental infirmity is due to old age and who do not require detention'. But by 1959, even including Old Park's full complement of forty-eight patients, the total number was down to 1209, and a general downward trend had begun.

This trend was probably not evident at the time. No great break-through is commented on in the reports, which continue to record the progression of Hospital life as they had done for a century.

- The Commissioners, though their 1956 report was 'very satisfactory', commented on the 'high figure of seclusion of patients in the disturbed wards ... due to overcrowding [and] nursing staff shortage. There was a 'difficulty of segregation', and secluded patients demanded the 'constant attention of nursing staff'.

*By permission of Joan Bradley*

**Ward Decorated for Christmas**

- Gordon-Russell gave a press interview to refute complaints against the Hospital which had been made in a letter published in the Daily Express. The Editor of the national newspaper expressed his 'profound regret' at having published it.
- Electric razors were purchased for patients' use.
- A quotation for tiling was received from 'Messrs Semtex Ltd' - probably quite a mundane name at the time, but hardly so in decades to come.
- Out-patient clinics were started at Chippenham and at Savernake Hospital, Marlborough.
- The Hospital farm had been closed, and all farming activities had ended except for pig-keeping, which itself did not survive for much longer. The demolition of farm buildings was 'necessary to provide a clear site for the new Admission/Treatment Unit'.
- Campfield, the Superintendent's residence, was too vast and rambling to continue in use as a modern family home. It was converted into single accommodation for the younger doctors, while Gordon-Russell and his family lived in Easedale, which up till then had been the Deputy Superintendent's residence.

*View of Roundway Hospital from Centenary Booklet, 1951*

*By permission of WRO*

# 18 - There they Stand

The Mental Health Act of 1959 followed a Royal Commission, on whose recommendations, in the Percy Report, HMCs had been consulted, including of course Roundway HMC. It made what Watkin calls 'a clean sweep of existing mental health legislation' and provided a single code for 'mental disorder', to cover both mental illness and mental deficiency. Admission to mental hospitals was freed from legal formality, but some powers of detention were retained, albeit with a right of appeal to a tribunal. There was to be a restoration of some mental health functions to the local authorities, which were to provide residential community after-care and diagnostic clinics. The Roundway HMC 'warmly welcomed' this, but regretted the demise of the Board of Control and of the 'cordial relationship' which had existed with its Commissioners. In anticipation of the Act, Gordon-Russell had started a programme of 'regrading of some 250 certified patients to Voluntary status', so that by 1959 there were virtually no certified patients.

One of the main principles of the 1959 Act, the Minister of Health said, 'is the re-orientation of the mental health services away from institutional care towards care in the community'. We see in this now familiar phrase the introduction of a concept that was to be the dominant theme in mental health generally, and for Roundway in particular, for the rest of the century. The mental hospitals were still seen as having a major role in the 1959 Act's concept of partnership with local authority community care, but a new Minister of Health, Enoch Powell, was soon to change that. The major implications of the widespread use of the new tranquillising drugs had in those two years begun to be recognised, and had led to new projections of the future needs for provision of mental health services. Powell announced in 1961 a policy of abolishing mental hospitals and cutting psychiatric beds by half within fifteen years, but with little promise of improvement in community services. There was still no sign of the specific grant to local authorities which the Percy Report had recommended, for capital development of these services. Most psychiatric patients, Powell said, would be treated in wards of general hospitals and not in 'great isolated institutions or clumps of institutions'. He continued:

> Now look and see what are the implications of these bold words. They imply nothing less than the elimination of by far the greater part

of this country's mental hospitals as they stand today. This is a colossal undertaking, not so much in the physical provision which it involves as in the sheer inertia of mind and matter which requires to be overcome. There they stand, isolated, majestic, imperious, brooded over by the gigantic water-tower and chimney combined, rising unmistakable and daunting out of the countryside - the asylums which our forefathers built with such immense solidity. Do not for a moment underestimate their power of resistance to our assault.

In describing 'some of the defences we have to storm' he spoke of 'erring on the side of ruthlessness', and referred to 'doomed institutions' and to 'setting the torch to the funeral pyre'.

It was perhaps just as well that the modernisation programme at Roundway that had been stuttering on for fifteen years was 'well nigh completed'. Its showpiece was the new Admission and Treatment Unit, named in 1962 after the recently deceased HMC vice-chairman Lady Katharine McNeile. A further modernisation programme was envisaged, but the financial climate can hardly have been favourable for it if closure was on the horizon. Even so, the anticipated reduction of in-patient numbers in the next fifteen years was rather less dramatic than the Powell statement had suggested; a reduction not by half but by less than one-third was foreseen, to 800 beds.

Keeping the patients actively employed was still considered a vital part of their treatment. The emphasis, which from the 1930s had shifted from work on the Hospital's internal services to occupational therapy activities, now moved further to include outside industrial work. In 1960, fifty-seven patients were working in building, agriculture, or making rubber mouldings. By 1963 the number in 'industrial therapy' had risen to 125, some of them assembling ball-point pens, while a further 373 were employed 'in wards and departments'; these patients were paid nominal amounts, but pocket money was paid also to 'indigent' patients who could not work. Occupational therapy was broadened to include art, pottery and drama, but more activities were sought, particularly for females. A major industrial therapy project was started in 1966 when Roundway opened a factory for making and packing chalk, converting for the purpose the former pig houses which had been out of use since pig-keeping had stopped five years before. It was a joint project with Messrs Harbutt's of Bath, who shared the setting-up costs with the Regional Health Authority. Within a year the factory was employing 300 patients, some earning the statutory maximum of two pounds a week, and Harbutt's were 'impressed' with the results.

Shopping days were introduced, when local firms were invited to bring a selection of their goods for sale to patients. In due course an outfitting department was set up on a more regular basis, though many had to be persuaded to buy and wear 'their own personal clothes'.

The frequency of entertainments offered to patients had fallen away somewhat, but its scope was widening. Concerts were fewer, but snooker exhibitions were more frequent, including one by the current World Champion, John Pullman, for which he was paid fifteen guineas. Carnival Days, Open Days and Garden Parties were held, and the Christmas programme was as packed and as elaborate as ever. Patients undertook a ten-mile sponsored walk. Coach outings were common, and a holiday at Southsea for selected patients became an annual event. Ronnie Newman wrote that:

\*　　\*　　\*　　\*　　\*

*While on holiday with some of the elderly patients, I drank a pint of 'mild' with Billy B — — who came to us in 1910, and rose from his bed every morning for 50 years to milk by hand our herd on the hospital farm. He had never been outside the gates in all those years until we took him on his first holiday in the late 60s.*

\*　　\*　　\*　　\*　　\*

Newman records several other anecdotes of individual patients, some of which show that sexual liaison between male and female patients was occasionally achieved, with ingenuity. The following are more appropriate for publication:

\*　　\*　　\*　　\*　　\*

*There was a little man whose favourite seat in the Male Infirmary Ward was on the heavy wood coal bunker. The lids of these bunkers were extremely heavy and when dropped the noise was equal to a double-barrelled gun report. This man had for someting like thirty years the delusion that he carried a monkey in his guts, as he described it. On this particular day he was by the bunker when it was dropped accidentally from the hand of an Attendant. The little man jumped several inches from the floor but most remarkable was his immediate reaction - he pointed to the 6" open window and exclaimed 'There the bugger goes'. He had seen the monkey fly through the window and though he lived for many years he never again complained of that monkey in his guts. Could this have been a case of Shock Therapy, a prelude to ECT in the future? Who knows?*

\*　　\*　　\*　　\*　　\*

*Another man in the same ward we knew as 'Plummy', his surname or Christian name were never used to the day he died. He had been committed from prison for putting a sleeper on the railway line at Swindon as a young man. He was an inoffensive little man and he did a life sentence as a certified lunatic for his crime. The sanitary arrangements in the Infirmary Ward were frightful, there was one lavatory for the ambulant, and there were few of these. All the bed patients used commodes and Plummy would rise from his bed at dawn and empty these commodes. In one hand he had his mouth organ which he was never seen without and in the other the revolting contents of the commodes. I doubt if he washed his hands all day, but he was never ill and died in advanced years.*

*   *   *   *   *

*The story of Ike is worth a mention. The temperature of his bath water was always wrong, either too hot or too cold, and then Ted Lake [the Attendant] used what was then an up-town word, saying 'That's tepid'. Ike looked at him and said 'Well, tis now too bloody tepid'.*

*   *   *   *   *

*In Male 6 I remember an elderly man, Bill, who was a professor type of individual and had his own library of books, but he will be remembered for his violin playing. He played from music but his tempo was so fast that looking over his shoulder, it seemed impossible that every note could be played at such speed, truly a remarkable and deeply interesting study for any Medical Superintendent. [Newman, it may be remembered, was himself a musician, and familiar with instrumental scores, if more attuned to trombone tempi.]*

*   *   *   *   *

*Then there was Ernest, who was in Male 2 (now Poplar Ward). This old man died [shortly after World War II] having been admitted as a young man. He had worked in the Great Western Railway Works at Swindon. Frank Norris, the Charge Nurse, had given him a side-room especially for his project to build a tank GWR locomotive and tender. This came to be the patient's life work for some thirty years or more. The whole was constructed of thick cardboard, cotton reels and strong thread, nothing more. Every day of his life in the ward he worked at it and when I entered the Service in 1934 he had completed it. He was quite an elderly man then but he serviced it until his death. It was about 7' or 8' long. Before Ernest died Frank Norris had retired and when the old man died this real work of art was taken to the tip and destroyed.*

*   *   *   *   *

Quotations were invited in 1970 for demolition of the cemetery chapel, burials in the cemetery having been discontinued four years before. In Newman's view the destruction of this chapel ranked with the destruction of Ernest's model locomotive as 'another instance of ignorance and official

By permission of Bill and Bridget Styche
*Ronnie Newman (standing) with male student nurses in their residence, Beavis Corner.*

vandalism'. He writes that in the cemetery bodies had been buried 'four to six in a grave, the first at twelve feet depth, then two feet of earth and a corrugated cover, etc'. Geoff Mascall, the son of a former chaplain to the Hospital, estimates that around 2500 people had been buried there since 1892. He is making a detailed study of the history of the burials in the Hospital Cemetery, about which he writes in Appendix 1.

The Hospital acquired its own coach. It was a gift from the new League of Friends of Roundway Hospital, which was soon to have branches at Calne, Melksham and Swindon, and was beginning to take a prominent role in the entertainment and welfare programme.

The relationship of patients to the medical staff was changing, largely due to the calming influence of the new drugs. They enabled the introduction of a Therapeutic Community approach, in which mental hospital patients, as Eric Pryor explains, 'were encouraged to take responsibility for their own behaviour'. Treatment was 'based on discussion rather than direction', with all staff levels as well as patients having an input. Wards began to be left unlocked, and the first mixed-sex wards were introduced.

About one quarter of the patients had permission to leave the Hospital grounds unsupervised; their ward was responsible for them, including their appearance. There was the occasional unfortunate incident, such as the patient who collapsed in a fit in the Rising Sun Inn in Devizes in 1964, and whose subsequent treatment by the Hospital drew a letter of complaint from the Ministry of Health: also the drunken patient who caused a disturbance by entering Southbroom Secondary Modern School in 1967. Reginald Buttery remembers that the people of Devizes were very kind to these parole patients, despite the stigma which they could never entirely dissociate from 'that place down Pans Lane'. In particular there was a good relationship with the shopkeepers, who would show restraint with any patient caught shoplifting. They would contact the Hospital, and Buttery, who was a JP, would arrange for a policeman to come and give the patient a dressing down, which 'rarely failed to work'.

*By permission of Gweneth Helliar*

**Hospital Retired Employees Outing 1966**

# 19 - Capacity for Independent Living

The Katharine McNeile Clinic, the first part of Roundway to adopt some of these new approaches, is described by a former patient as 'very well got up - just like a beautiful hotel', and the treatment regime 'absolutely brilliant', but it was not long before it ran into difficulties. Complaints about the catering were recorded in 1966, and by 1969 had reached such a pitch that 'a multi-signature complaint had been forwarded by the Patients' Committee to the Prime Minister'. Neither was the building itself entirely sound. 'Plaster faults' put the dining room and main lounge out of commission in 1970, only eight years after the Clinic had been opened, causing 'a serious interruption of hospital treatment', and soon after there was claimed to be 'a general deterioration of "atmosphere" ... not entirely due to the plaster failure'. The building had to be evacuated, and repair work took several months.

Further disquieting events assailed Roundway about this time. In 1968 there were press reports criticising the management of the Hospital, and the HMC minutes of the time confirm that there was serious friction between medical staff and management. Careful wording, and even the deletion of one relevant entry, fail to shroud the vehemence with which the doctors aired their grievances, including demands for closer consultation over development proposals. The HMC was briefed by one of its consultant psychiatrists on 'the dehumanising atmosphere of a certain ward ... [which] could actually produce "Disturbed Patients" and adversely affect staff'. Roundway was 'lagging behind' in its nurse/patient ratio, in staff training, and in numbers of consultants and medical staff. The HMC blamed inadequate funding from Region.

In the midst of this the admission to Roundway of a twelve-year-old boy caused widespread concern after local and national media reporting, including a feature on Harlech TV. Reginald Buttery, who was Chief Male Nurse, remembers the boy as 'very, very disturbed and extremely violent', though 'lovable' in between his frequent attacks. Roundway 'didn't normally take that kind of patient', but 'agreed to take him because he was in our area'. He improved and settled down with drug treatment, and was eventually moved to a more appropriate hospital. The incident revived earlier unsuccessful efforts to persuade the Regional authority to provide Roundway with an adolescent unit.

A programme was established by the mid-1960s to take a more measured approach to the rehabilitation of patients for transfer to care in the community. Its aims were 'to prevent and reverse the worst effects of institutionalisation, encourage progress, however slow, towards capacity for independent living, ... [and eventually] to transfer to a rehabilitation unit'. Bill Greenaway recalls that, in the first years after the Powell measures were introduced, mental hospitals had been under pressure to release to the community as many as ten per cent of their patients per year, often with woefully inadequate preparation and disastrous results. Such a pace was, mercifully, not maintained. Reports in 1966 and 1967 foresaw a more modest reduction of overall numbers, with smaller, mixed wards and special psycho-geriatric units, while a dedicated rehabilitation facility, the Wyvern Unit, was opened in 1967. Some of the staff houses in the Hospital grounds were converted as half-way houses for patients being prepared for community life, but some difficulty was experienced in finding suitable outside lodgings for them. Though there was still some overcrowding, the number of resident patients did begin to show the expected steady decline. Helped by increasing numbers being treated at the Seymour Clinic in Swindon and the Bath Psychiatric Unit, by 1970 the number resident at Roundway had reduced to 886, the lowest figure of the century.

Two houses were acquired in Swindon in 1973, for 'patients being returned to the community', and four patients moved into the first of them in September of that year. A Rehabilitation Committee was by 1974 meeting regularly at Roundway, in the hope of improving co-ordination between social workers and nursing staff. Sometimes the Hospital was given (presumably by its

*By permission of Bill and Bridget Styche*
*Opening of Nurse Training School. Reg Buttery, Alderman R. Kemp (HMC Chairman),*
*Mrs J Westwater, Bridget Melody, Dr J. S. Westwater (SW Regional Hospital Board)*
*and Miss E. J. Tomkinson (HMC Vice Chairman).*

Regional masters) as little as four weeks to prepare a group for community life, though two to three months was a more normal period, and some needed as much as six months. A quota system appears once again to have been operating; an 'objective' in 1975 was to move thirty patients out in the coming six months, followed by a further sixty. In addition to group houses, lodging schemes were initiated, though not without some difficulty. Following a survey of some 500 apparently suitable houses by 'sociology students attached to the social workers here', sixty-five potential hosts expressed interest and were invited to the Hospital, but only four turned up, and only two of these 'started visiting the wards'. It was quite a milestone in the project when the first Devizes landlady was found in 1976.

According to Enoch Powell's plan, 1975 was the year by which mental hospital beds would have been virtually eliminated. But a Department of Health and Social Security report admitted that there had been failures as well as successes. Mental hospitals had not disappeared. Kathleen Jones summarises, in *Experience in Mental Health*, that by then:

> Though overcrowding had been reduced and resident populations had decreased, no single hospital had closed. It was forecast that 'some hospitals will continue in use for many years'. Staffing levels were often 'less than adequate' and amenities lacking. Community facilities would need to be built up 'from their present minimal level', and there was a note of warning about the limits of public tolerance - the demands made on the community 'must not be greater than the community can accept'. There was little hope of 'the kind of service we would ideally like even within a twenty-five year planning horizon'.

Despite this admission, which Jones assessed as 'profoundly depressing', the authors of the DHSS report believed that 'the failures and problems are at the margin', that 'the basic concept remains valid', and that 'the philosophy of integration rather than isolation which has been the underlying theme of development still holds good'.

A further NHS re-organisation in 1974 had been experienced with mixed feelings at Roundway. The HMC had been disbanded and, though six of its members were co-opted by the Bath Area Health Authority committee which would oversee the Hospital, it was seen as a further stage in the inexorable movement away from the family atmosphere of the past, much of which had been lost when the last Superintendent left ten years before. Both Gweneth Helliar and Reginald Buttery express regret at these developments, the latter with some force; 'Bath would supervise us by telephone - a sorry state of affairs'. Nursing services were also affected by the changes, new designations and re-gradings inevitably leading to some bitterness. An early move by the new administration was to divide the Hospital into two distinct sectors, one dealing exclusively with patients from the Swindon health district and the other, slightly larger, with those from Bath. Certain wards were allocated to each sector, and patients placed accordingly, as an aid to their eventual return to the community in their own area.

In the mid-1970s Roundway became the host to the Devizes Hospitals Broadcast Service, broadcasting to all the hospitals in the Devizes area. It moved its studio into the basement of Roundway's main block, after a few years of operating in Roundway village. BBC Wiltshire Sound broadcaster James Harrison relates that he began his broadcasting career there, along with several others who have since built successful careers in the media, both in Wiltshire and further afield. Though the basement studio was near the hub of the central heating system, and therefore extremely hot, Harrison felt that when the studio was relocated to the newly revamped Beavis Corner building, even with better facilities all round, it had lost some of its charm.

A *Roundway Hospital Profile* produced by Bath District Health Authority in 1979 gives a snapshot, at least from the official point of view, of the situation at that time. Roundway had:

- 600 patients.
- Training provision for a 'comprehensive range of psychiatric nursing'.
- Rehabilitation Units including 'a purpose built dwelling offering complete independence before final discharge to the community, several group homes and a hostel ward'.
- Several psycho-geriatric wards, backed up by Day Hospitals in local towns.
- A Continuing Education Department, which offered 'Study Days/Workshops' for staff.
- Acute admission wards, incuding a Mother and Baby facility.
- 'An active Rehabilitation Work Centre for patients' employment' [referring mainly to the chalk factory].
- The Tomkinson Centre; the patients' licensed Social Club, providing indoor and outdoor activities, further education classes, occupational therapy, live entertainers, dancing and social events.

Dr George Lodge, a consultant psychiatrist who arrived in the same year and was to be at Roundway until its closure, recalls, however, that at that time, well into the second decade of the rehabilitation policy, there were still incomplete resources and inadequate funding for the process. The therapeutic team for the Bath sector of the Hospital claimed in 1983 that 'thirty per cent of patients could leave hospital tomorrow if services were provided'. But Lodge was looking for effectiveness rather than speed, and was determined that the preparatory process for rehabilitation would be made more thorough during the 1980s. A selected group of patients would set up a 'home' within the Hospital, and receive life-skills training from occupational therapists. Once a home in the community was available for them, they would themselves choose materials and colour-schemes for it, and help to prepare it for occupation. Social workers would visit the new household frequently, and the resettled patients would continue to attend as day-patients, either at Roundway or at one of their local clinics.

Committee minutes in Lodge's early years at Roundway record his involvement, even before he took the Chair of the Medical Advisory Committee early in 1984, in a range of matters. He reported in December 1979 that a patient had built himself a 'house' in the Hospital grounds and would not return to sleep in the ward, and advised that there was less risk in leaving him there than forcing him back to the ward. He was unhappy with a general agreement in 1983 that 'there should be a withdrawal of OT [occupational therapy] services throughout the hospital, particularly in the long stay wards' - it was already apparent that with fewer patients it was becoming harder to sustain a worthwhile recreation programme. But he did agree with the findings of a Hospital Advisory Service report in the same year, which advised development of the Hospital shop, improvement of the psychotherapy service, and more training for junior doctors in ECT, while complaining of too much night sedation of patients and very low morale among nurses.

Reginald Buttery, who retired soon after Dr Lodge arrived, has misgivings about the success of rehabilitation. Many, he feels, were sent out too quickly and with inadequate preparation. For some years after discharge they would be seen 'roaming around lost'. They might be 'pushed out to some landlady who is an "eight-to-six" woman', where they would get little care, and since 'they couldn't supervise their tablets, they got no medication'. One patient, discharged against his will and without preparation after twenty years at Roundway, was sent back by his GP within two days, and committed suicide the following day. Buttery's negative view of the changeover to a care in the community policy is echoed by former Hospital Secretary Bill Styche, and also by Bill Greenaway, who feels that the resources devoted to the process were, and are, 'completely inadequate', and that the 'halfway house' programme was 'like a net with a hole in it'.

Gweneth Helliar, on the other hand, thinks that on the whole the rehabilitation programme was very successful. Her recollection is that the preparation process could take up to two years. Though patients 'stood out like a sore thumb' when first placed in the community, they adapted within months so that 'you couldn't tell them from anyone else'. She had assisted in enabling the rehabilitation of some long-stay patients about whom very little was known, including some wartime evacuees to the Hospital, by conducting a survey of their backgrounds. But she shares some of the criticisms expressed by Buttery, Styche and Greenaway, feeling in particular that in the case of 'really institutionalised people', there were not enough community care staff to supervise them in the vital matter of taking their drugs.

**Patients at work in the Industrial Therapy Unit**

# 20 - Nobody's Baby

A new Mental Health Act in 1983 was claimed to be a 'patients' charter with new civil rights provisions'. But some found it too legalistic for staff to work with, and Kathleen Jones dismisses it as 'a diversionary activity ... [which] does little or nothing to help patients in hospital, and the many thousands out in the community'. Patients' rights were to be safeguarded by revised admission and discharge procedures and stricter regulations as to consent to 'irreversible or hazardous' treatments, the local authority social services role was stepped up, and a Mental Health Act Commission was established, with similar inspection functions to the old Board of Control and its predecessors. The Commission, even though its members served only part-time, was seen by Eric Pryor as the 'most important innovation' of the Act, and its visits are virtually the only evidence of the Act in Roundway records. On their 1987 visit they found a patient who had been kept in seclusion too long for their liking, and recommended improvements to the seclusion room; a heater, lockable window, door with armoured glass in place of the peephole, externally operated lighting, and an 'unhangable' ceiling'.

The charity MIND had taken a prominent role in the movement leading to the 1983 Act, and was also making practical contributions to the rehabilitation process at many mental hospitals. For Roundway patients, MIND assisted in providing resettlement homes, often in partnership with Housing Associations and with other charities, and set up Friendship Clubs for ex-patients in several Wiltshire towns.

The Team for Assessmemt of Psychiatric Services (TAPS) made a study in the late 1980s of patients who had left two mental hospitals in the London area on rehabilitation. Dylan Tomlinson's *Utopia, Community Care and the Retreat from the Asylums* summarises the results. The Team castigated the 'unfulfilled promise' of support services outside the hospitals, which were 'barely in evidence'; 'the new health centres, the accessible "walk-in" refuges, the new forms of domiciliary care, the new work opportunities, and the new leisure activities'. Nevertheless they concluded that 'the outcome did bestow many benefits on the people who moved in the early years of reprovision'. Resettlement was not a cure, however:

Patients moving out of hospital do not become any less 'mad' or any more 'able', at least in the clinician's view, one year after moving out to the community. But once resident in their community placements, 'leavers' very much preferred the setting to that of the hospital.

What former patients liked most was the greater freedom (far better than even the open, unlocked wards which had for some years been the norm), and having sampled it many soon wanted to move on from their placements. The study found little evidence of public concern about resettlement of the mentally ill, except when a group home was proposed in their 'back yard'; there was no equivalent in mental health of the general habit of protest against hospital closures.

Around 1987 a weekly lunch club was started in Devizes for former Roundway patients who had been resettled in the local community. Known as the All Seasons Club, it has run continuously ever since, with a programme of outings and social events for its members, most of whom are living as near normal lives as possible in supported group homes in Devizes. Some were willing to talk about their recollections, with a mixture of feelings but generally favourable, except for one moan about the food. One recalls that he underwent both insulin and ECT treatment; he feels that he benefitted from both, but does recount the horrifying experience of waking up from the anaesthetic while in the throes of ECT convulsions. He expressed regret that Roundway is not still in being. In recent years the All Seasons Club has been run by Catherine Leigh, who worked at Roundway for 28 years, and who expresses generally positive views of the rehabilitation process.

Sir Roy Griffiths, in his widely debated 1988 report, *Community Care: Agenda for Action*, said that community care was 'a poor relation: everybody's distant relative, but nobody's baby'. The Department of Health admitted in their response the following year that:

> There are legitimate concerns that in some places hospital beds have been closed before better, alternative facilities were fully in place, … [and that] … at times, patients have been discharged without adequate planning to meet their needs in the community. … Ministers will not approve the closure of any mental hospital unless it can be demonstrated that adequate alternatives have been developed'.

Ministers must have been happy that such conditions existed in Roundway's case, since it is clear that within a month of the publication of that report a closure plan was a *fait accompli*. In addition to Swindon and Bath, plans had existed since 1987 to accommodate both elderly and acutely mentally ill patients in community hospitals at Marlborough, Melksham, Chippenham,

Westbury and Trowbridge. A proposal to close Roundway 'and build a new acute unit on another site' had been under consideration at least since 1988, and the January 1990 minutes refer to 'the building of the new psychiatric unit at Roundway in 1996'. What was meant by 'at Roundway' was a site of '9.6 acres in a triangle near the Katharine McNeile Clinic', which was allocated in 1992 for 'relocation of acute and rehabilitation facilities', a reference to what became Green Lane Hospital. It was important that 'the present main building has to have a view', presumably for getting the best price for selling to developers.

Hospital services had been gradually running down for some years; the falling numbers tended to make their upkeep uneconomical. The Tomkinson social centre had been under threat of closure as early as 1981, when there were still nearly 600 patients. In 1987, with the number around 450, physiotherapy services were cut back, and leisure activities were at a low ebb. The League of Friends of Roundway Hospital was nonetheless doing its best, reporting that:

> Many of our friends among the residents had gone into the community so our outings have been very much curtailed. We had however managed trips to Longleat, Cotswold Wild Life Park, daffodil picking, the Mayor's Carol Concert and visits to friends and relations for tea.

Despite the earlier agreement to withdraw occupational therapy services, a level of service was still being provided through to 1992, when barely 200 patients were resident, and indeed was continued right up to the closure of the Hospital. The cleanliness of the Hospital, rarely if ever questioned in the past, was 'not as good as it was'; in 1986 it was noted that 'Moore Ward smells', and that domestic staff had had to be called 'to remove faeces from stairs in the main hall'; some areas in 1989 were 'in a disgusting state'.

On the positive side, however, a market garden was opened in 1986, in cooperation with the Shaw Trust, of Devizes, and was providing valuable therapy for thirty patients in 1989. An article in *Growth Point* magazine gives some detail:

> Ironically, the [market garden is] surrounded on two sides by fields (now leased to a farmer) that were once part of the farm run by the hospital and its patients - until Ministry of Health directives in the 1950s and 1960s decreed that farmland should be dispensed with unless proven to be of 'sustantial' therapeutic value to patients. ... The bulk of the garden produce, which includes most kinds of vegetables and several soft fruits (from 500-600 bushes), is sold to the catering department of the hospital. ... Among the welcome animal species are the geese and ducks, kept in a large outdoor pen.

It is explained that 'many patients feel a need to do productive work', and the case is quoted of a patient who had been seventeen years at Roundway and who gained such benefit from a year working in the garden that he found a job and moved out to a hostel. This is all highly reminiscent of the nineteenth century belief in the benefits of such work to patients, since subordinated to artificially constructed Occupational Therapy programmes.

For several years, some wards had been undergoing modernisation, including 'cubiclisation', while others, despite lobbying by the Friends of Roundway Hospital, had been closed or adapted as office space. But from 1992 onwards, ward closures became a one-way process as alternative facilities throughout Wiltshire became available. Five wards were closed during 1993 with the loss of more than a hundred beds.

The Katharine McNeile Clinic, which had been 'under-used' in 1982, was adapted to prolong its life, with various new roles. But as a result, a returning patient, who had warm memories of a spell of treatment there twenty years before, now found herself in far less congenial surroundings in the main building, where acute, short stay patients could no longer be insulated from the most institutionalised long-stay patients of either sex. She would occasionally see patients being brought in 'handcuffed to policemen', which may be surprising for the 1990s, but is consistent with a provision of the 1983 Act that a mentally ill person could, exceptionally and with a magistrate's warrant, be removed to a 'place of safety', accompanied by a social worker, a doctor and a constable.

# 21 - The Pendulum Swings

The history of Roundway Hospital, under that name and earlier as Wiltshire's county mental hospital or its lunatic asylum, is the nationwide history of the treatment of mental illness in micrososm. Generally, Wiltshire followed, and often even lagged far behind, what the rest of the country was doing, though very occasionally it was among the leaders.

In the 1840s, when pauper lunatics were gathered from the workhouses into the new asylums, to be 'cured' by kindness, morality and wholesome occupation, Wiltshire appointed as their Medical Superintendent one of the most progressive mental health practitioners of the day in John Thurnam. As the early optimism was dissipated in mounting numbers and bureaucracy, Thurnam was succeeded, briefly, by a bungler and then by a rising youngster destined for the rarified heights of the Lunacy Commission. Throughout the long period when no better hope could be offered than containment of an

Photograph by P Steele

*Roundway Hospital under conversion to private dwellings, 1998.*

escalating problem, two highly worthy if uninspiring gentlemen, John Ireland Bowes and Sydney Cole, made a thoroughly competent job of not allowing things to get much worse.

Cole, however, with his successor John Leech in the 1920s, did ensure that Wiltshire was in the forefront of the opening up of mental health treatment elsewhere than in the monolithic mental hospitals, by starting out-patient clinics. This could be regarded, with hindsight, as the seed which germinated into care in the community. Leech also introduced Electro Convulsive Therapy, which was to achieve lasting if qualified success in treating some forms of mental illness, and several other physical treatments which were not. But it was Millar Speer, the last of the figurehead Medical Superintendents, followed by J B Gordon-Russell, the sole Physician Superintendent, who were in control when the major tranquillising drugs became widely available in the late 50s and early 60s. It was this development which set the trend of patient numbers on a downward path, both nationally and at Roundway, where the number had peaked at over 1500. In its turn, this trend offered the government a solution to the problem of maintaining or replacing the rambling old, outdated asylums, by transferring the great bulk of the patients from medical care in hospitals to social care in the community.

Though under-funded - seriously so at first, by the government's own admission - the process of rehabilitation, begun in the 1960s, continued to a point where the mental hospitals, Roundway among them, could be closed. The undoubted fact is that many patients were rushed into the outside world with distressing effects, and many practitioners of the time look back on the process with dismay. But studies which consider the balanced picture have found wide measures of success to set against these shortcomings. It must surely be better to have, as we now do, a range of education programmes, supervised homes, and out-patient treatments, which allow large numbers of people to live their own lives in normal surroundings, who might otherwise have been consigned to an all-embracing sink-hole for the mentally ill, by whatever bland euphemistic title it may be known. On the other hand, the pendulum seems to have swung too far, so that there is no haven (asylum?) or constraint for the dangerous social psychopath, and the law is likely to be tight-ened in the hope of reducing the number of homicides committed by the mentally ill from the 1998 level of one per week.

As regards Roundway itself, what did it feel like to be there? Conversations with those who were familiar with the Hospital in its later years convey a mix of views. In general terms, the longer their involvement and the higher their position in the heirarchy, the more favourable their impressions. Medical, administrative and senior nursing staff generally recall a happy and reason-ably bright place, albeit with some frustrations and a feeling of remoteness from the controlling authority. Shorter-term employees and visitors to patients, on the other hand, tend to recall with greater emphasis the first depressing impact of a community of exiles from society in surroundings of gloom and hopelessness, with unpleasant smells and an air of impending delapidation. There is an indication here that, not surprisingly, familiarity with the place and responsibility within its management process could blunt the impact of the less happy aspects of the institution which might appal the lay person. It is probable that, for the same reasons, the official records tend to gloss over much that was dreary, frightful and forbidding. Even so, on the balance of these conversations, the author is left with a clear impression of dedicated and benevolently motivated teams doing their best over the decades, sometimes in adverse circumstances, to improve the lot of their unfortunate charges.

The final few months of Roundway Hospital saw the available beds reduced to eighty, with several of them vacant, and Green Lane Hospital being built in a corner of the grounds as its small-scale successor. Of the treatments used in earlier years, ECT remained 'the most effective for severe depression', but was needed less due to the 'increasing range of psychotropic drugs'. Seclusion, a fall-back since 1851, was not absolutely out-dated; a new policy for its use had been agreed in 1994. The last few patients were transferred to Green Lane on 25 October 1995, and Roundway was closed. Some features of the old hospital were incorporated in Green Lane, mainly light and space, high ceilings and open plan, which had tended to be lost during 'modernisation'. Planners of the new hospital, as George Lodge related, had found that an uncrowded environment, where people could find their own space and not feel hemmed in, led to a lower level of disturbance. He said, 'If you put people in a good environment they will behave well'. John Thurnam had said something similar in 1851.

# Appendix I

## Roundway Hospital Burials

*By Geoff Mascall*

The Cemetery at Roundway Hospital was in use from 1852 to 1966 and probably contains some 2,500 burials, the overwhelming majority being patients from the hospital. To date some 1300 names have been transcribed from the burial book to a more manageable database.

Nothing now remains of the once well kept grass, paths and numbered marker bricks that showed this sloping field was once in use. It was the closure of Roundway Hospital and this anonymous patch of overgrown weeds and grass that prompted the work of assembling the names of all those interred with a view to ensuring their existence is recorded for those who search for long lost relatives.

My association with Roundway Hospital had begun when I was six in 1955 when my late father became Chaplain to the hospital. As a small child I well remember visits to the Hospital and the unrestrained affection shown by the patients to a small frightened boy. Perhaps it might be possible, in some small measure, to repay their kindness by my researches, to help ensure each individual might be remembered. My grateful thanks to Phil Steele for the opportunity to outline some of my findings in his book.

The cemetery was located between the cricket field and Drews Pond Lane, on a south facing slope. The small chapel built around 1852 was demolished around 1968. Burial plots followed a single path that ran from the north-west corner of the field to the then arched gateway opening onto Drews Pond Lane, the path then ascending the slope and curving towards the north-east corner and the cricket field.

The much modified hospital is now a housing estate encroaching closer and closer to the cemetery, perhaps one day to be swallowed up by pressure for more housing or to become part of the amenities of the estate. It would perhaps be most fitting that these gentle people might lie beneath a child's playground.

Sadly all the numbered grave markers were removed by an overzealous grass cutter whose mower kept hitting them when cutting the grass and stacked by one of the walls so each individual plot location has been lost. Fortunately a sketch map has survived and although not to scale it does give a good insight into the position of each plot, many of which hold four or five bodies.

The majority of patients buried in the cemetery seem to have come from Wiltshire, mostly from Union Workhouses, some from private addresses, some from other hospitals, some from police stations or prisons such as Broadmoor, a few found wandering at large, a few directly from London and other centres of population, one in 1927 from the Great Western Railway Coffee Tavern, Swindon.

All occupations, where mentioned, seem to be represented; signalmen, quarrymen, domestics, doctors, nurses, farm labourers, shoe makers, painters, unemployed, naval pensioners, discharged soldiers, paupers, militia drummer, coachbuilder, engine driver, school mistress, hawker and costermonger. Some 10% of entries have an occupation: most state 'Lunatic Asylum, late of...'

The following chart, for the 60% of the burials so far transcribed, is of Recorded Age at Death, the top row indicating the tens of years, the left hand column the individual years. Matching the vertical and horizontal column and row gives the number of burials for the corresponding age group: for example to discover the number of burials for those aged 56 the column headed 50 and the row 6 gives the figure of 18 burials; conversely 29 burials were for those aged 76. The greatest age at death was 94, the youngest two twelve year olds save two still births and 10 unknowns.

| Age | 0 | 10 | 20 | 30 | 40 | 50 | 60 | 70 | 80 | 90 |
|---|---|---|---|---|---|---|---|---|---|---|
| 0 | | | 2 | 4 | 16 | 21 | 17 | 39 | 23 | 4 |
| 1 | | | 3 | 4 | 11 | 15 | 35 | 42 | 24 | 4 |
| 2 | | 2 | 6 | 12 | 14 | 26 | 28 | 46 | 12 | |
| 3 | | | 5 | 12 | 20 | 20 | 24 | 42 | 17 | 1 |
| 4 | | 1 | 8 | 7 | 11 | 18 | 22 | 35 | 17 | 1 |
| 5 | | 2 | 8 | 13 | 22 | 24 | 26 | 24 | 10 | |
| 6 | | 1 | 6 | 9 | 13 | 18 | 29 | 29 | 10 | |
| 7 | | 3 | 6 | 17 | 10 | 23 | 39 | 24 | 10 | |
| 8 | | 3 | 4 | 11 | 18 | 11 | 38 | 19 | 10 | |
| 9 | | 2 | 7 | 14 | 23 | 27 | 35 | 21 | 2 | |
| Still birth | 2 | | | | | | | | | |
| Unknown | 10 | | | | | | | | | |
| Totals | 12 | 14 | 55 | 103 | 158 | 203 | 293 | 321 | 135 | 10 |

*Roundway Hospital: Age at Death Synopsis (1304 deaths 1898 to 1966)*

# Appendix II

## Chronology of Wiltshire Asylum
## Wiltshire County Mental Hospital
## Roundway Hospital
## 1845-1995

1845    Lunatics Act places on county authorities the duty of providing accommodation for 'Pauper Lunatics and Idiots'.

1848    Wiltshire Quarter Sessions approves erection of an asylum to accommodate **250** patients. Site and architect's plan approved by Secretary of State.

1849    Construction starts. Dr John Thurnam, from the progressive York Retreat, appointed Medical Superintendent.

1851    Building completed. First patients admitted 19 September.

1856    Building of new ward agreed, due to overcrowding on female side.

1858    New female ward opened.

1860    **350** patients in residence.

1863    Patients take part in procession in Devizes to celebrate wedding of Prince of Wales.

1863-66 Three more wards added - two on female side, one on male.

1869    Wiltshire has highest incidence in the country of both paupers and pauper lunatics.

1870    **449** patients.

1873    Death of Dr Thurnam. Dr James Wilkie Burman appointed to succeed.

1874-75 Adverse press reports: Burman's attitude to working patients 'monstrous', empty coffin burial, attendant convicted for assaulting patient.

1877    Two more wards added, one for females and one for males, the latter to double as entertainments hall.

1878    'Round Robin' complaint by attendants. Burman resigns; replaced as Medical Superintendent by Dr Edward Marriott Cooke, aged twenty-six.

1880    **587** patients.

1881    Cooke resigns, to become Superintendent at Worcestershire Asylum. Dr John Ireland Bowes succeeds.

c1881  'Wet-pack' treatment introduced.

1886    Idiots Act introduces distinction between mental handicap and mental illness, and encourages special provision for 'idiots' and 'imbeciles'. Wiltshire sees no need - refuses approach from neighbouring counties to make joint provision.

1888    Isolation ward built, separate from main building. (It was never used as such, but became a detached Villa-type ward.)

1889    Control of Asylum passes to new Wiltshire County Council.

1890    **674** patients.

1890s  Various building projects to increase capacity. Third storey added to main building, and a second storey to Villa ('Isolation') ward.

1891    Wiltshire's proportion of lunatics to population has relatively improved to only fifth highest in the country, though overall incidence of insanity thought to be increasing.

1892    Superintendent's house 'Campfield' built adjacent to main building.

1898    Recreation Hall added, plus Engine Room to enable conversion from gas to electric light.

1900    **916** patients.

1904    A second Villa added.

1901-06 Ratio of attendants/nurses to patients improved over past twenty years from 1:13 to 1:9. Reductions in escapes, and in use of restraint and seclusion, over same period.

1906    To ease overcrowding, some 'harmless' patients being discharged to workhouses and some patients boarded out to Dorset Asylum.

1908    A suicide - the first in the Asylum for twenty-four years.

1910    **976** patients.

1913    Dr Bowes retires; suceeded as medical Superintendent by his deputy, Dr Sydney Cole.

1913-14 Building of new Annexe started but halted due to war.

1914    Ninety evacuee patients received from Bristol Asylum - shortage of staff at all levels due to war service.

1915-16 Death rate doubles, mainly due to TB and dysentery in overcrowded wards.

1917    200 evacuee patients received from Portsmouth Asylum. Number of patients peaks at **1131**.

1919    Evacuee patients returned to Bristol and Portsmouth.

1920    **919** patients.

c1920   'Prolonged bath' treatment supersedes wet-pack.

1920s   High levels of TB and dysentery persist. Inspectors critical of sanitary and welfare standards.

1922    Name changed to Wiltshire County Mental Hospital.

1924    Building of Annexe completed after wartime hold-up. 110 patients imported from home counties to allow it to be operated efficiently.

1927    Out-patient clinics started in Swindon by Dr Cole and in Trowbridge by his deputy, Dr John Leech.

1927    Nurses' Home built. Sister-Tutor appointed to conduct in-house training.

1928    Occupational Therapy introduced.

1930    Mental Treatment Act introduces categories of 'voluntary' and 'temporary' patients. The terms 'asylum' and 'lunatic' no longer used. Out-patient clinics and employment of social workers encouraged.

1930    Two social workers appointed.

1930    **1144** patients.

1934    Cole retires; succeeded by Leech.

1935    Major building and reorganisation scheme approved, to increase patient capacity and improve sanitation, with TB and dysentery still persistent. (But the start was delayed long enough for the war to cause indefinite postponement.)

1937    Proportion of voluntary patients reaches one-third.

1937    Hospital Chapel completed and dedicated.

1938    Malarial therapy and drug-induced convulsive therapy introduced.

1939    220 evacuee patients received from Hampshire.

1940    **1411** patients.

1941    Sixty-seven more evacuees received, from Surrey and Hampshire.

1942    Electro convulsive therapy (ECT) introduced. Seventy-six patients treated.

1943    Patient number reaches all-time peak of **1510**.

1946    Pre-frontal leucotomy introduced.

1947    Leech retires; succeeded by his deputy, Dr Millar Speer.

1948    Introduction of National Health Service. Control transferred from local government to Ministry of Health. Name changed to Roundway Hospital.

1948    Modernisation and reorganisation project given Regional Hospital Board approval after thirteen years of delay, but little practical progress.

1950    **1321** patients.

1951    Seventy wartime evacuee patients still present.

c1952   Insulin coma therapy introduced.

1954    Continuous bath equipment removed.

1956    Opening of Old Park House as annexe for (eventually) forty-eight elderly female patients.

1956-59 Introduction of the major tranquillising and anti-depressant drugs, heralding first sustained reduction in patient numbers.

1957    Speer retires as Medical Superintendent. Dr J B Gordon-Russell succeeds him, designated Physician Superintendent. Gordon-Russell extends use of ECT.

1959    Mental Health Act frees admission to mental hospitals from legal formality, and restores some functions (eg after-care) to local authorities. The Act aims to re-orientate mental health services away from institutional care towards care in the community.

1959    Gordon-Russell regrades 250 certified patients to voluntary status; virtually no certified patients at Roundway after this date.

1960    Industrial therapy started; fifty-seven patients in outside employment.

1960    **1142** patients.

1961    Minister of Health Enoch Powell announces policy of abolishing mental hospitals.

1962    Admission and Treatment Unit opened, named Katharine McNeile Clinic.

1962    League of Friends of Roundway Hospital founded.

1964    Gordon-Russell leaves. Superintendent post discontinued.

1966    'Chalk factory' opened on site as industrial therapy project. 300 patients soon employed there.

1966    Last burial in Hospital cemetery.

c1968    Therapeutic Community approach adopted, giving suitable patients more freedom and involvement. Wards begin to be unlocked; some mixed-sex wards introduced; annual holiday to Southsea introduced.

1968    Friction between medical staff and management; recorded in minutes and reported by press.

1969    Admission of a twelve-year-old boy draws media criticism.

1970    **886** patients.

1973    First patients returned to the community; housed in Swindon.

1974    Rehabilitation Committee starts regular meetings.

1974    NHS reorganisation; has unsettling effect on management and nursing at Roundway.

1976    Hospital divided into Bath and Swindon sectors, to aid rehabilitation.

1976    First Devizes landlady found for rehabilitated patients.

1980    **585** patients.

1983    Mental Health Act aims to safeguard patients' rights with revised procedures for admission, discharge, and consent to treatment.

c1983    The charity MIND begins assistance with Roundway's rehabilitation process.

1980s    Falling numbers lead to gradual run-down of support and welfare services. Cleanliness suffers.

1986    Market garden opened, provides therapy for thirty patients.

1987    Plans to accommodate mental patients in community hospitals throughout the County.

1989    Department of Health admits inadequate planning for community care.

1989    Decision taken to close Roundway.

1990    Plans for a new small psychiatric hospital in a corner of the Roundway grounds - to become Green Lane Hospital.

1990    **270** patients.

1993    Selective refurbishment of wards ends. Five wards closed, reducing beds by more than 100.

1994    ECT remains an effective treatment. Seclusion still an option, under new rules.

1995    The last patients transferred to Green Lane Hospital on 25 October. Roundway Hospital closed.

# SELECT BIBLIOGRAPHY

## Wiltshire and Swindon Record Office (WRO)

| | |
|---|---|
| A1/570/1. | Minutes of Court of Quarter Sessions, 1846-51. |
| A1/572. | Petition against establishment of Asylum. |
| A1/576. | Papers on mental health, from 1830s. Census Returns. |
| F1/100/11 series. | Minutes of Committee of Visitors, from 1885. |
| J4/110 series. | Annual Reports of Committee of Visitors, Medical Superintendent, Chaplain, and Commissioners in Lunacy, from 1851. |
| J4/111 series. | Visitors' Report Books, from 1876. |
| J4/113/1. | Centenary Booklet, *Roundway Hospital, Devizes, 1851-1951* (Devizes: Wiltshire Gazette, 1951). |
| J4/160/2. | Regulations for Visitors (19th Century, undated). |
| J4/161/1. | Photographs of Superintendents and Committee Members. |
| J4/162/1. | Autobiographical notes (unpublished) by RK Newman. |
| J4/174/1. | Journal of Admissions and Discharges, from 1879. |
| J4/190 series. | Male Patients' Case Books. |
| J4/191 series. | Female Patients' Case Books. |

## Wiltshire Archaeological and Natural History Society (WANHS)

Annual Reports of Medical Superintendent for various years between 1937 and 1955, including some not held at WRO.

*Roundway Review* (Roundway Hospital Management Committee), monthly, c1952 to 1958.

Jane Bayley, 'Garden Therapy at Roundway', in *Growth Point*, Winter 1989/90, pp8-9.

Sydney John Cole, *Autobiography* (unpublished: 1941).

John Leech, *Inside-Out - The View from the Asylum* (self-published: 1995).

John Leech, *The Lunatic Years* (self-published: 1992).

Peter McCree, 'The Institutional Response to Insanity in Nineteenth Century Wiltshire', in *Wiltshire Archaeological Magazine* vol 84 (1991) pp96-107.

Barry M Marsden, 'John Thurnam', in *Popular Archaeology*, July 1981, pp25-6.

Stuart Pigott, 'John Thurnam (1810-1873) and British Prehistory', in *Wiltshire Archaeological Magazine* vol 86 (1993) pp1-7.

The Cunnington Scrapbooks: Article from unnamed newspaper by William Morris of Swindon, 1886. Article from *Wiltshire Gazette*, 9 July 1903.

## Secondary Sources

Pat Barker, *Regeneration* (Harmondsworth: Penguin, 1991).
Colin Briden, 'John Thurnam, 1810-1873', in P V Addyman and V E Black (eds), *Archaeological Papers from York* (York Archaeological Trust, 1984) pp163-5.
Joan Busfield, *Men, Women and Madness* (Basingstoke: Macmillan, 1996).
David Buxton, *Devizes Voices* (Stroud: Chalford Publishing Co, 1996).
David Buxton and John Girvan, *A Devizes Camera II* (Devizes Books Press, 1986).
Pamela Colman, *Devizes in Old Picture Postcards* (Zaltbommel, Netherlands: European Library, 1983).
Courtney Dainton, *The Story of England's Hospitals* (London: Museum Press, 1961).
Kathleen Jones, *Experience in Mental Health - Community Care and Social Policy* (London: SAGE Publications, 1988).
Kathleen Jones, *Asylums and After* (London: Athlone Press, 1993).
John Pollock, *Shaftesbury, the Poor Man's Earl* (London: Hodder & Stoughton, 1985).
Roy Porter, *English Society in the Eighteenth Century* (Harmondsworth: Penguin, 1990).
Roy Porter, *Mind-Forg'd Manacles* (Harmondsworth: Penguin, 1987).
Lindsay Prior, *The Social Organisation of Mental Illness* (London: SAGE Publications, 1993).
Eric H Pryor, *Claybury, A Century of Caring* (London: The Mental Health Care Group, Forest Health Care Trust, 1993).
R B Pugh and Elizabeth Crittall, *The Victoria County History of the Counties of England - Wiltshire vol V* (Oxford University Press, 1957).
Andrew Scull, *Social Order/Mental Disorder* (London: Routledge, 1989).
Andrew Scull, *The Most Solitary of Afflictions* (Yale University Press, 1993).
Dylan R Tomlinson, *Utopia, Community Care and the Retreat from the Asylums* (Milton Keynes: Open University Press, 1991).
Brian Watkin, *Documents on Health and Social Services, 1834 to the Present Day* (London: Methuen, 1975).

## Journals

Jonathan Andrews, Review of Bernard Cashman, *A Proper House: Bedford Lunatic Asylum 1812-1860* (North Bedfordshire Health Authority, 1992), in *The Local Historian*, vol 23 no 3, pp178-180.
Jerome Burne, '750 years of Bedlam', in *Rx*, 5 October 1997, pp13-14.
Michael Gray, 'George Maton (1820-1900)', *News, No 3* (The Merchant's House (Marlborough) Trust, Dec 1991), p11.
Geoff Mascall, 'Burials at Roundway Psychiatric Hospital, Devizes', in *Wiltshire Family History Journal*, October 1998, pp45-6.
Peter Nolan, *Bulletin of History of Nursing No 12* (University of Birmingham, 1987), pp 18-21.
Roy Porter, 'Bethlem/Bedlam - Methods of Madness?', in *History Today*, vol 47(10), October 1997, pp41-47.